The Basic Book of

Woodworking

Patrick E. Spielman

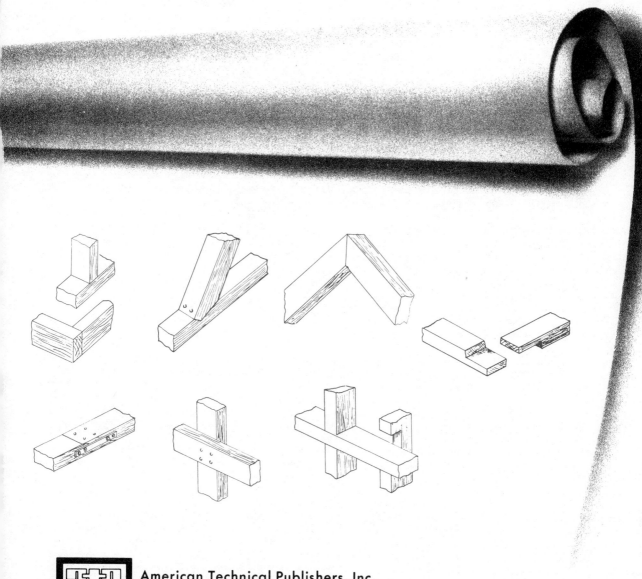

American Technical Publishers, Inc.
Alsip, Illinois 60658

COPYRIGHT© 1979

BY AMERICAN TECHNICAL PUBLISHERS, INC.

Library of Congress Catalog Number: 78-78182
ISBN: 0-8269-4810-3

No portion of this publication may be reproduced by any process
such as photocopying, recording, storage in a retrieval system or
transmitted by any means without permission of the publisher

123456789-79-98765432

To my family for their patient understanding, and especially to
my lovely wife Pat who's work and support is immeasureable.

PRINTED IN THE UNITED STATES OF AMERICA

CONTENTS

1   page 1   **Introduction**

Unit 1   2   Skilled Woodworkers
Unit 2   4   Safety
Unit 3   6   Planning a Project
Unit 4   10   Materials
Unit 5   13   Measuring and Marking

2   18   **Cutting to Size and Shape**

Unit 6   19   Handsawing
Unit 7   24   Portable Saber Saw
Unit 8   26   Jigsawing
Unit 9   30   Basic Band Sawing
Unit 10   34   Special Band Saw Jobs
Unit 11   38   Hand Planes
Unit 12   41   Block Planing
Unit 13   43   Hand Drilling and Boring
Unit 14   46   Portable Electric Drilling
Unit 15   49   Drill Press Drilling and Boring
Unit 16   52   Chiseling and Gouging
Unit 17   54   Filing and Rasping
Unit 18   56   Portable Electric Routing
Unit 19   60   Tool Sharpening

3   64   **Smoothing**

Unit 20   65   Sandpaper
Unit 21   67   Hand Sanding
Unit 22   70   Portable Electric Sanding
Unit 23   72   Sanding Machines

4   75   **Fastening**

Unit 24   76   Joints
Unit 25   79   Gluing and Clamping
Unit 26   82   Nailing
Unit 27   85   Wood Screws

5   88   **Finishing**

Unit 28   89   Wood Finishing
Unit 29   93   Hardware

6   96   **Advanced Woodworking Machines**

Unit 30   97   Table Sawing
Unit 31   101   Planing on the Jointer
Unit 32   104   Using the Surface Planer
Unit 33   106   The Lathe
Unit 34   110   Turning Spindles
Unit 35   115   Face Plate Turning

7   117   **Wood and Wood Materials**

Unit 36   118   The Nature of Wood
Unit 37   122   Wood Sheet Materials

8   124   **Projects**

   134   **Glossary**
   136   **Index**

PREFACE

THE BASIC BOOK OF WOODWORKING is part of an integrated series of Industrial Arts textbooks designed to teach basic skills to beginning students. Its major objectives are career exploration, developing consumer awareness, manipulative skills, and craftsmanship. The philosophy of THE BASIC BOOK OF WOODWORKING is based on a recent, nationwide survey in which woodworking teachers at all levels were asked to outline the courses they taught and let us know what types of instructional materials they actually needed. The result is a highly-visual text with a controlled reading level that will help insure student success.

The authors and the publisher wish to acknowledge and thank the following individuals, agencies, and corporations for their assistance and cooperation: American Forest Products Industries Inc., Dunbar, American Plywood Association, Long Bell, Behr-Manning, U.S. Plywood, Glen Barquest and Wilfred Pierick (University of Wisconsin-Extension), U.S. Forest Products Laboratory, Spielman's Wood Works, Indian Archery, Skill Corp., Rockwell Tools, Greenlee Tools, Stanley Tools, Milwaukee Electric Tool Corp., Black and Decker, Borden Co., Adjustable Clamp Co., Deft Inc., General Finishes, Watco-Dennis Corp., and Brodhead-Garrett.

Thanks also go to Mark Bogenschutz, Mike Franke, Todd Schreiber, Bob Spielman, Greg Swain, and John Wehling for constructing and testing projects.

The Publisher

INTRODUCTION

1

Imagine, if you can, a world where there is no wood.

The pencil on your desk would be nothing more than a piece of graphite. But, then, there wouldn't be a desk. Or a chair. Maybe not even a floor. Chances are that the roof over your home would be gone too. This book wouldn't exist. Paper, as you know, is made out of wood pulp.

Whatever you do in the future will somehow be connected to wood. Suppose you want to build your very own home. Of course you'll use cement and steel and glass. But you'll use more wood than any other single product.

If you become a designer of stereo components, you'll have to know about wood for cabinets. Become a gunsmith and discover fine woodworking in gunstocks. The owner of a shoe store or shoe repair shop will have to deal with fancy wooden heels.

Finely worked pieces of wood are sold as jewelry and sculpture.

Expensive imported automobiles advertise their real wood paneling. Good sets of pots and pans have natural wood handles. Even the lowly toothpick is made of wood.

Architects and engineers study the structural use of wood. Fuels and plastics are made from wood by chemists. Farmers and nutritionists are trying wood as an animal feed supplement.

Besides the hundreds of thousands of carpenters, cabinetmakers, furniture makers, millwrights, and lumberjacks who make their livings directly from wood, there are millions more people whose jobs are directly linked to wood products.

Think of the people who make chain saws and chisels, table saws and hatchets, logging trucks and sandpaper.

A woodworker can have custom built furniture—or even gain fame as an artist or scientist. Some people work outdoors as home builders or in factories as furniture makers. As a student of woodworking you can make, use, and enjoy the products of your own skill, practically within weeks of starting to learn woodworking.

Woodworking can be a career or a hobby, but it is always useful. No one knows the pride of quality work as well as the professional or amateur woodworker.

Wood is a natural material. Each piece is different and people want to touch it (figure 1-1) as well as see it. There is a special pleasure in seeing and touching wood that has been worked by a skilled woodworker (figure 1-2).

What the beginning student gains from a course in woodworking is:

● Safety—a knowledge of how to be safe when working with wood

● Skill—the ability to make tools and wood cooperate

● Experience—the how to do it knowledge gained from actually working with wood

● Appreciation—pleasure of fine wood and woodwork

Figure 1-2: The work of a professional wood carver shows mastery of basic hand tool skills as well as artistry. (U.S. Forest Products Lab)

Figure 1-1: Wood appeals to both the sense of sight and touch. It is this double appeal that makes wood unique. (U.S. Plywood)

Figure 1-3: Skills learned in basic woodworking will be valuable to the students the rest of their lives. (Spielman's Woodworks)

Figure 1-4: Simple skills learned on small projects will work just as well on bigger projects.

Figure 1-5: Knowledge and experience is necessary to turn many projects that look easy into reality. Because of the way a bow is constructed for strength as well as beauty it is an advanced project. (Indian Archery)

Figure 1-6: Simple woodworking skills are enough to build a house—if they are thoroughly learned.

Working safely and taking care of the shop requires everyone's help. The school shop is like a small factory. Part of being professional is being safe—both in school and in industry.

Skill is taught in projects. They involve the same materials and tools used by all skilled professional woodworkers. Sawing, planing, shaping, fastening, and finishing wood are just some of the things you will learn.

Experience in simple woodworking will have future benefits (figure 1-3).

Skills learned now may be used in advance classes to build furniture (figure 1-4), sports gear (figure 1-5), or even small buildings (figure 1-6).

Appreciation comes from doing. Using wood and learning to work with it develops an appreciation for other woods and other people's skills.

SELF CHECK

1. List four things that are taught in woodworking.
2. What does safety require from every student?
3. How does a school shop differ from a factory?
4. What kinds of skills are taught by woodworking?

All work in the shop must be done with everyone's safety in mind. The most important safety tool in class is a good attitude. The right attitude simply means being a good worker. When doing something, consider the other people in the shop.

There are five important areas of safety:
- Personal safety
- Eye protection
- Tools
- Housekeeping
- Materials storage and handling

Horseplay in a shop filled with dangerous tools is "grade school stuff." Running, pushing, or hitting is dangerous to the people doing it. But it is also dangerous to someone across the shop who might look up—and cut himself with a saw or chisel.

Personal safety includes clothes. Loose fitting clothing like sweaters, jackets, ties, and jewelry should be taken off. Shirt tails and long hair must be tucked in. Sleeves should be buttoned or rolled above the elbows (figure 2-1). Wear shop aprons. Report all injuries, even the slightest scratch, sliver, or cut.

Figure 2-1: Working safely. Notice the safety glasses, shirt tails tucked in, sleeves rolled up, and the guards in place.

NEVER MONKEY AROUND machinery or tools you don't understand!

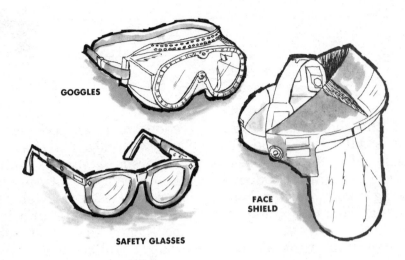

GOGGLES

FACE SHIELD

SAFETY GLASSES

Figure 2-2: Three types of eye protection.

Eye protection is required for power tool work (figure 2-2) or where there is flying dust or particles. Tool safety means not touching or handling a tool until your instructor demonstrates the safe and correct way to use it, and gives you the "okay". Use the right tool for the right job. Carry sharp tools carefully (figure 2-3). Always cut away from your hands and body. Clamp your work in a vise whenever possible. Close vises when they are not in use. Return tools to their proper place. Do not use tools with cracked or loose handles. Do not cut with dull tools.

Housekeeping means cleaning up and caring for the shop. Sweep up scraps that someone might slip on. Avoid spilling glues, oils, or finishes. Close lockers, doors, and drawers, and keep aisles clear.

Good material storage and handling prevents fires. Shavings, dust, solvents and dirty rags must be stored in the proper containers.

Figure 2-3: Carefully carry sharp edge or pointed tools with the points and cutting edges down.

SELF CHECK

1. List five areas of safety in the shop.
2. What is the first tool safety rule?
3. Why is loose clothing a safety hazard?
4. What safety precautions should be taken to protect your eyes?

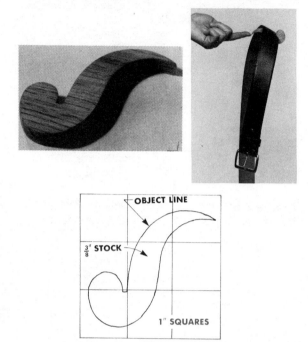

Figure 3-1: The magic belt hanger starts as an idea. Once it is obvious how it works, it is turned into a pattern.

Your first project should be quick and easy to complete. Getting skilled with hand tools takes longer than becoming skillful with machines and the best project is one that won't be rushed.

The order for planning a project is:
- Select project (figures 3-1 to 3-9)
- Make desired changes
- Do a working drawing

Project plans can be made either bigger or smaller. They also may be changed for another use. For instance, the ski rack (figure 3-6) may be changed into a tennis racket rack (figure 3-7), a mug rack (figure 3-8), or a clothes rack.

After getting approval from your instructor for a project, a drawing of the project must be made. A complete drawing or sketch gives the size, shape, and location of every part. A drawing giving all of the information needed to

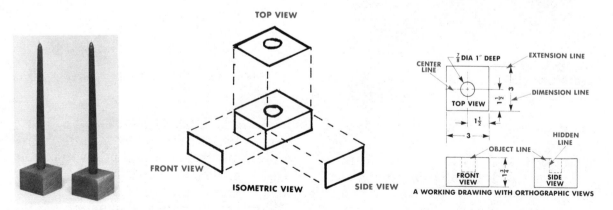

Figure 3-2: A candle holder is entirely different from a belt hook. But the steps for turning it into a project are the same.

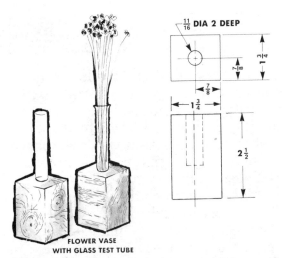

Figure 3-3: Desired changes must be made while the project is being drawn. It is easier to make changes with a pencil than with a saw.

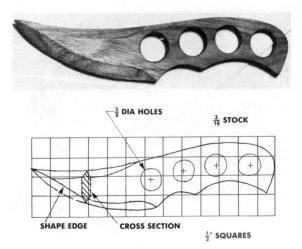

Figure 3-5: Note the cross section which shows the shape of both sides of this letter opener.

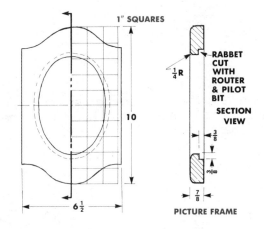

Figure 3-4: This frame for a 5x7 photo might be needed for an 8x10. To make the change, alter the dimensions of the drawing.

make a project is called a <u>working drawing</u>.

The <u>grid system</u> helps you draw to proportion. A drawing of a project that has irregular curves usually has squared lines drawn over it (figures 3-1, 3-4, and 3-5). The grid system of squares is used to enlarge patterns or irregular shapes to full size. The process is easy. First draw the right size and number of squares as given on the drawing. The squares may be drawn directly on the wood, but they are usually drawn on paper. The paper is later used with carbon paper or cut out and traced onto the wood.

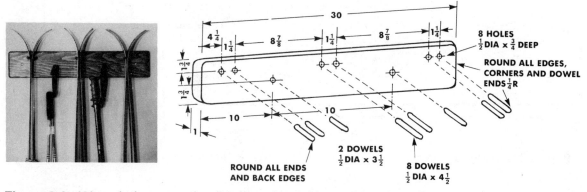

Figure 3-6: Although these are the directions for making a ski rack, a little thought and a few changes to the drawings can make it into something else.

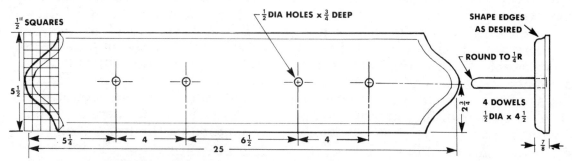

Figure 3-7: The tennis racket holder is simply a modified ski rack.

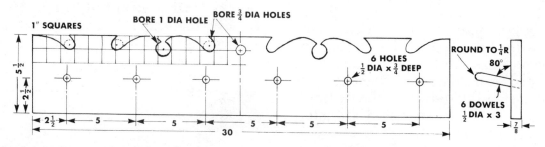

Figure 3-8: This mug rack has the same design and construction elements as the ski rack in figure 3-6.

To draw the full-sized shape, mark each grid line where the line of the desired shape crosses it. Mark only one square at a time. Connect the marks lightly to reproduce the shape. Then smooth out the curves and darken the lines.

Methods of telling size (the scale of a drawing) are important because most drawings are not made full size. A scale

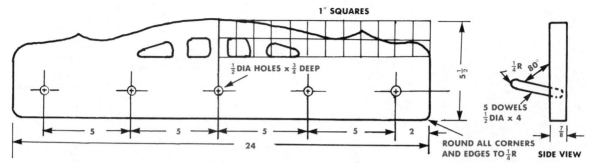

Figure 3-9: By looking closely, it is possible to see how a ski rack can become a clothes rack.

drawing is usually drawn smaller than the actual size. Full size dimensions are given on the drawings even though it has been made smaller. Scale drawings are used with the grid system and most working drawings. Lines and numbers are added to the drawing so it is possible to read the size. Measurements are usually given in inches. The symbol (") which means inches is left off. Other symbols you will find on drawings are:
● R which means radius
● DIA which means diameter
● ° which means degrees

Each line of a drawing has a special job. Object lines are dark. They show the outline or shape of the project. Dimension lines are thin with arrows at each end. A number near the center of a dimension line tells you the distance between each arrow tip. Extension lines are thin lines that make it possible to move the dimension line away from the object line (figure 3-2).

A center line is a light broken line of long and short dashes. It is used to show the center of a round object. Holes in wood are located by two center lines. They cross at the center of the hole.

Hidden lines are light, broken lines of short dashes. They show the edges of the object that are hidden from view. Hidden lines also show round or square holes (figures 3-2, 3-3 and 3-4).

Extra views are often necessary to clearly describe the project in a drawing. Rectangular objects are often drawn with three views (figure 3-3). When two views are identical or one of the views is not necessary, one can be eliminated (figures 3-2 and 3-3).

Section drawings (figure 3-4) show the inside of a part as it would look if it were cut apart. The cut surfaces are marked with slanted lines drawn closely together. Note the sectional view in figure 3-5.

SELF CHECK

1. Why should a first project be small?
2. What does a working drawing have on it?
3. How is a grid system used?
4. List the three basic lines used in working drawings.

Figure 4-1: Lumber or boards come in three forms: rough, surfaced 2 sides (S2S), or surfaced 4 sides (S4S).

Figure 4-2: Worked lumber or mouldings come in a variety of shapes.

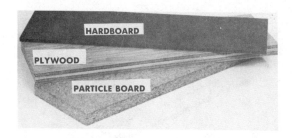

Figure 4-3: Plywood, hardboard, and particle board are the usual wood sheet materials.

Once a project has been selected and drawn, wood is needed to make it. There are many kinds of wood to use (See Units 36 and 37). But the beginning student should use the wood the teacher recommends.

Wood used in shops usually comes as:
● Lumber or boards (figure 4-1)
● Worked lumber or mouldings (figure 4-2)
● Sheet materials such as plywood (figure 4-3)

Lumber and boards are either rough or surfaced. Hardwoods are generally bought as S2S (surfaced 2 sides) lumber. Softwoods are usually S4S (surfaced 4 sides). Woods may be tested for hardness by pressing a thumbnail into a scrap (figure 4-4).

Basic board terms describe the dimensions and surfaces of lumber (figure 4-5). Dimensions are given as thickness, as width, and as length. Length always runs with the grain and may be shorter than width.

Lumber is sold by board feet. A board foot is 1 inch thick, 12 inches long, and 12 inches wide of rough sawn lumber. This is equal to 144 cubic inches (1"x12"x12"=144") (figure 4-6). After measuring, the board is dried and surfaced. The finished dimensions of a board foot of S4S lumber are 3/4 inch thick, 11-1/4 inches wide, and 12 inches long (figure 4-7).

Figure 4-4: Woods may be tested for hardness by gouging them with a thumbnail.

<u>Rough sawn lumber</u> contains 144 cubic inches of wood per board foot. S4S lumber has approximately 101 1/4 cubic inches of wood per board foot.

To find the number of board feet in a piece of wood, change all dimensions to inches:

$$T'' \times W'' \times L'' = \text{Board feet}$$

In order to figure the price of a piece of rough sawn wood 1 inch by 6 inches by 48 inches at \$1.65 a board foot, the procedure is:

$$1'' \text{ (T)} \times 6'' \text{ (W)} \times 48'' \text{ (L)} = 288$$

$$\frac{288}{144} = 2 \text{ board feet}$$

$$2 \text{ (board feet)} \times \$1.65 = \$3.30$$

<u>Worked lumber</u> includes dowels, mouldings, and special shaped boards. These materials are sold by the linear or running foot. A linear foot is anything that measures 12 inches in length (figure 4-8):

$$\frac{L''}{12} = \text{linear feet}$$

<u>Sheet materials</u> include panels of plywood, hardboard, particleboard, and other sheet materials such as plastics.

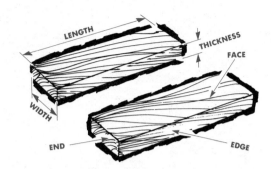

Figure 4-5: When describing wood, length always runs with the grain.

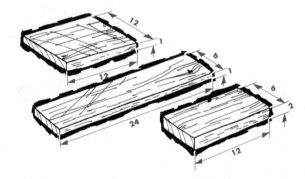

Figure 4-6: A board foot may be any shape, but it always contains 144 cubic inches of rough sawn wood.

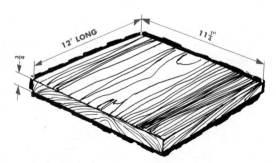

Figure 4-7: Because wood is sold by the board foot (rough sawn), a finished board foot is smaller than an unfinished board foot.

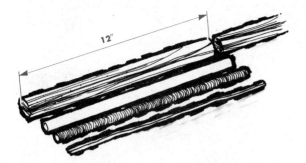

Figure 4-8: A linear foot is anything that measures 12 inches in length. Dowel rod, pipe, and lamp cord are sold by the linear foot.

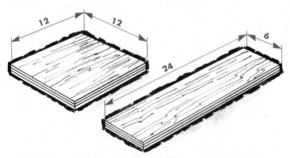

Figure 4-9: Sheet material is sold in square feet. Sheet material should measure exactly the dimensions it is sold at.

| BILL OF MATERIALS | | | Student's Name *Sandy S.* | | |
| | | | Project *clothes rack* | | |
Part Name	Kind of Material	No. of Pieces	Finished Size from Drawing	Cost Per Foot	Part Cost
Back	Pine	1	7/8 x 5½ x 24	70¢	70¢
Dowels	Birch	5	½D x 4"	9¢ per ft.	15¢
			Finish		25¢
			Sandpaper + Glue		25¢

NOTES:
1. Add ½" to width and 1" to length of back
2. Avoid knots
3. Cut dowels to finished length
4. Add 25 cent finishing cost
5. Add 25 cent glue and sandpaper cost

ESTIMATED COST $1.35

ADJUSTED COST $1.50

Sheet materials are available in different thicknesses. The most common sheet size is 48 inches by 96 inches (4 x 8 feet). Sheet material is sold by the square foot or by the sheet (figure 4-9). A square foot is 144 square inches (12"x12"=144"). To find square feet:

$$\frac{W'' \text{ (width) x } L'' \text{ (length)}}{144'' \text{ (one square foot)}} = \text{square feet}$$

A bill of materials (figure 4-10) must be made before a project can be completed. It contains the information given on the drawing. It lists the number of pieces and kind of material for every part. Prices per part may be estimated at the same time.

Actual cost of a project is usually higher than estimated for several reasons. Sometimes the board width available is greater than you will need, or the wood must be cut oversize to allow for finish work.

SELF CHECK

1. List the three basic groups of wood materials.
2. What is the size of a rough sawn board foot?
3. What is the size of a surfaced board foot?
4. What is the difference between a board foot, square foot, and linear foot?

Figure 4-10: This is a typical bill of materials.

To make parts for a project the parts have to be measured and marked for cutting. Marking is done with a very sharp pencil. Don't use a ballpoint pen. The ink will seep into the wood.

Measuring begins with reading inches and fractions. Measuring and layout tools are divided into inches (figure 5-1). Most woodworkers use a tape measure which is marked to sixteenths of an inch (figure 5-2).

Normally rulers are 1 foot long. Two foot bench rulers are 24 inches long. Some 6 foot folding rules and tapes number the inches from 1 to 11. The twelfth inch is marked as "1 ft.". The thirteenth inch is marked 1-1, meaning 1 foot 1 inch.

It is better to measure with a long ruler once. Moving a short ruler several times may cause an error.

After taking measurements, lines have to be drawn. The most common line problems are:
- Squaring a line
- Drawing a straight line
- Gaging a line

Squaring a line is done with a try-square, combination square, or framing square (figure 5-3). To square a line the handle is held along one edge of the board. A line is then drawn along the blade with a sharp pencil.

A straight line is drawn between two points by lining a steel ruler up between them. The ruler on a combina-

Figure 5-1: This is how to measure and mark to length with a bench rule.

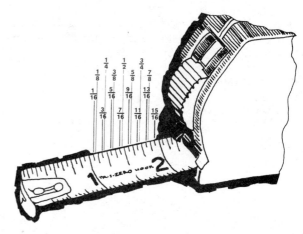

Figure 5-2: A tape measure is usually marked in 1/16 inch divisions.

tion square or one edge of a carpenter's framing square may be used.

Gaging a line is done with a combination square (figure 5-4). In gaging a line, the line is run parallel to the

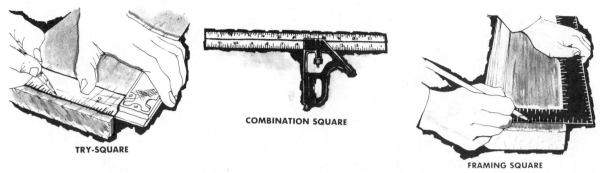

Figure 5-3: Lines can be squared with a try-square, a combination square, or a carpenter's framing square.

Figure 5-4: The combination square is used to gage a line parallel to the edge of a board.

Figure 5-5: A line can be roughly gaged using your finger as a guide.

edge of the board. A line may be roughly gaged using only fingers and a pencil (figure 5-5). Many tools are used for marking and checking measurements (figures 5-6 to 5-11).

Templates are also used to draw lines. A template is cut to the exact size and shape of a part. It is laid on the wood and outlined with a pencil (figure 5-12). Half-templates are used where the pattern can be split exactly down the middle and both sides are the same (figure 5-13). The half-template is turned over to draw both sides.

Metric measurements do not have fractions. There are one hundred centimeters (cm) to one meter, and ten millimeters (mm) to one centimeter (figure 5-14). Most measurements are given in millimeters.

Woodworkers should have no trouble with metric measurements. By using

Figure 5-6: The combination square can be used to make 45° angles.

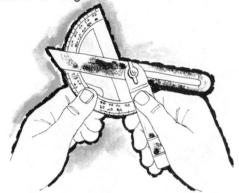

Figure 5-7 (A): A sliding T-bevel can be set to any angle.

Figure 5-7 (B): Using the sliding T-bevel to check a bevel cut.

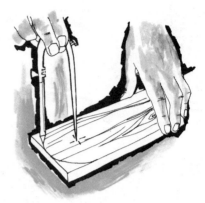

Figure 5-8: The wing compass is used to mark a radius.

Figure 5-9: Marking a board with a carpenter's framing square.

a metric ruler and measuring exactly, metric plans go together just like plans drawn in inches.

The desk set in figure 5-15 is dimensioned in millimeters. The only thing to remember is always measure with a metric ruler.

<u>Accuracy</u> makes good projects. An old-time carpenter's adage is, "measure twice and cut once." The reason is that a piece can be marked again if there is a mistake in measuring. But a piece cut wrong can only be thrown away.

Sharp, crisp <u>layout lines</u> that are measured accurately and checked twice

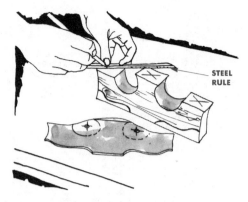

Figure 5-10: Note the use of corner to corner diagonals to find centers.

Figure 5-11: A scratch awl is handy to mark pieces.

Figure 5-12: Templates are laid on the wood and outlined.

will result in good looking woodwork. Careless or sloppy layout work makes careless and sloppy woodwork.

SELF CHECK

1. Why isn't a ball point pen used for marking wood?
2. List three kinds of squares.
3. What is a template?
4. How do metric projects differ from other woodwork?

Figure 5-13: If both sides of a pattern are exactly the same, a half template can be used to draw both sides. Just turn it over.

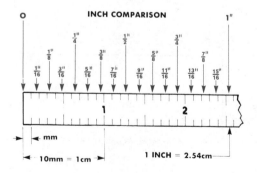

Figure 5-14: Metric measurements are easier because they don't have fractions.

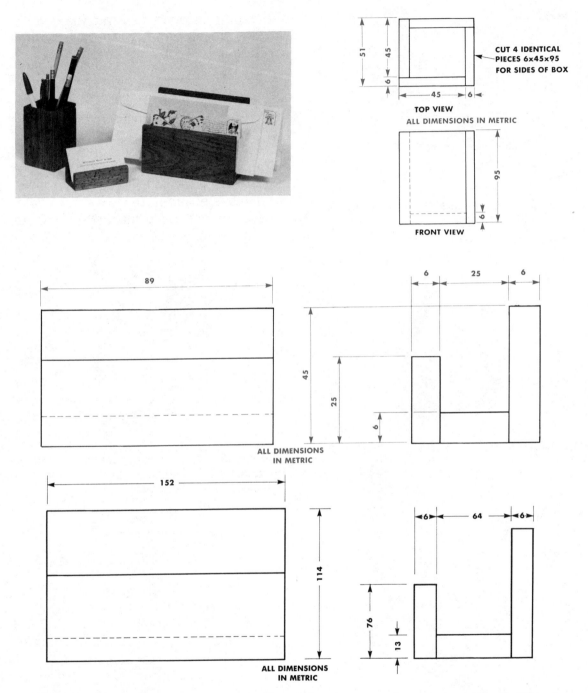

CUT 4 IDENTICAL PIECES 6x45x95 FOR SIDES OF BOX

TOP VIEW
ALL DIMENSIONS IN METRIC

FRONT VIEW

ALL DIMENSIONS IN METRIC

ALL DIMENSIONS IN METRIC

Figure 5-15: It is not necessary to convert metric to English measurements and back. All designs can be measured in one system only. Just don't forget and measure 13 inches when you want 13 mm.

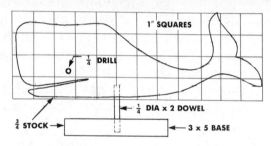

1" SQUARES

¼ DRILL

¼ DIA x 2 DOWEL

¾ STOCK

3 x 5 BASE

WHALE in natural pine can be sawn by hand or with the jigsaw or band saw. Try shaping the edges with files and sandpaper to get a more sculptured look.

Practically any woodworking project must be cut to size and shape. When you know how to cut and shape one board accurately, you will have the basic skills required to build anything from wood.

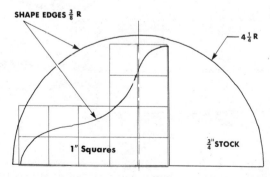

SHAPE EDGES $\frac{3}{8}$ R

$4\frac{1}{4}$ R

1" Squares

$\frac{3}{4}$" STOCK

SHELF of walnut stained pine. Use hand tools to shape the edges. Assemble with finish nails and glue.

HANDSAWING

Handsaws the woodworker uses most to make straight cuts are (figure 6-1):
● Crosscut saw
● Rip saw
● Backsaw
● Dovetail saw

The most important differences between saws are the teeth (figure 6-2). Teeth come in different sizes and shapes. But all saw teeth are set or bent to alternate sides (figure 6-3). Set this way, the teeth cut a groove that is wider than the saw blade.

Crosscut saw teeth have knife-like points designed to cut across the grain.

The grain in wood looks like fine straws glued together (figure 6-4). Wood length is measured with the grain, and crosscut saws cut across the

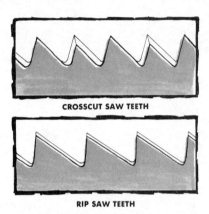

CROSSCUT SAW TEETH

RIP SAW TEETH

Figure 6-2: The differences between saws are in the teeth. Crosscut saws have knife-like points. Ripsaw saws have teeth like a row of chisels. Saw teeth may also be very fine or very coarse.

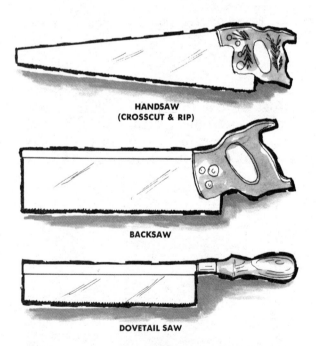

**HANDSAW
(CROSSCUT & RIP)**

BACKSAW

DOVETAIL SAW

Figure 6-1: The most used saws in woodworking are the standard handsaw with either crosscut or rip teeth, the backsaw, and the dovetail saw.

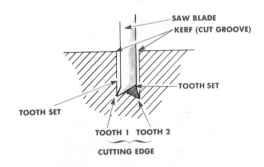

SAW BLADE
KERF (CUT GROOVE)
TOOTH SET
TOOTH SET
TOOTH 1 TOOTH 2
CUTTING EDGE

Figure 6-3: Although the teeth of a saw are no wider than the saw, they are bent to cut a groove that is wider than the saw blade. Thus the first tooth may be bent to the left, the second to the right, the third to the left and so on. Making the groove (or kerf) wider than the saw prevents binding.

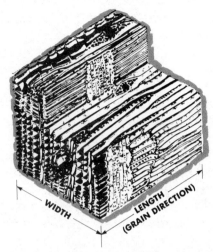

Figure 6-4: Wood fibers resemble bales of straw. Splintering occurs when these fibers are pulled loose instead of being cut. (Forest Products Lab)

Figure 6-6: The kerf is started with a backward cut. The saw may be lifted off the wood and reset at the board edge several times to repeat the backward starting cut if needed. Pushing the saw forward without a good kerf may cause the saw to jump out of the groove or damage the edge of the board by splintering it.

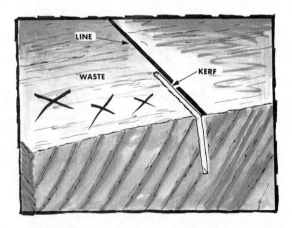

Figure 6-5: The saw cut or kerf is always on the waste side of the line. If the piece is too long it may be finished down to size. If it is too short, there is no way to stretch it.

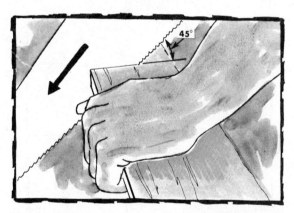

Figure 6-7: The forward stroke when crosscutting is done at 45°. This angle produces the cleanest cut and kerf.

grain, thus crosscutting means sawing to length.

Ripsaw teeth resemble a row of chisels (figure 6-2). Ripping is cutting with the grain. So ripping also means cutting the board to width.

The backsaw is similar to a regular handsaw. It has a reinforcing strip of metal on its back edge and is shorter.

The dovetail saw is even shorter than the backsaw. It, too, has a strip of metal on the back edge. But its teeth

Figure 6-8: Ripping also has its best angle. The saw should be held at 60°.

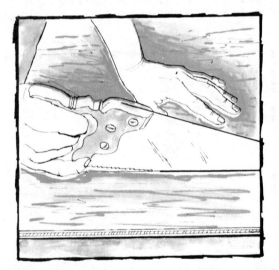

Figure 6-9: Because of the crossed grains in plywood it must be cut at a low angle of about 15°. This means the saw is held almost level with the wood. Sawing this way helps prevent splintering.

on the waste side of the cutting line (figure 6-5).

To make a straight cut, start the blade on a backward stroke. Guide the saw with your thumb (figure 6-6). After the kerf is started on the backstroke, the saw blade may be pushed forward at an angle of 45° for crosscutting (figure 6-7) and an angle of 60° for ripping (figure 6-8). Plywood is cut at about 15° (figure 6-9).

If the kerf starts to wander from the line, a slight twist on the saw will

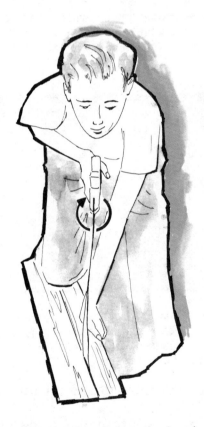

Figure 6-10: A slight twist on the handsaw will cause the blade to turn as it cuts. This twisting motion will bring the kerf back to the line if it starts to wander.

are much smaller and it is used only for fine finish work.

Saws leave grooves called <u>kerfs</u> in the wood. The kerf should always be

Figure 6-11: The loose end of a board being cut needs to be supported. Without support, it will break off and damage the cut piece of wood.

Figure 6-12: A square is used to check the cut.

bring it back (figure 6-10). When the cut is almost through the wood the loose end must be supported (figure 6-11). The wood end will break off in the final sawing if it isn't supported. The finished cut is then checked with a square (figure 6-12).

Very accurate crosscutting is done with a <u>miter box</u> (figure 6-13). The miter box holds the saw square to the wood at an exact angle. Most miter boxes use the back saw.

<u>Cutting curves</u> in wood is done with the coping saw (figure 6-14). The blade may be inserted into the wood through a drill-hole and then attached to the handle. In this way a hole may be cut in a whole piece of wood (figure 6-15).

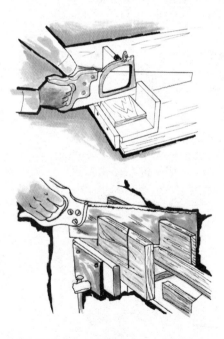

Figure 6-13: The miter box is a mechanical method of making an accurate cut. The frame that holds the saw may be adjusted to the needed angle.

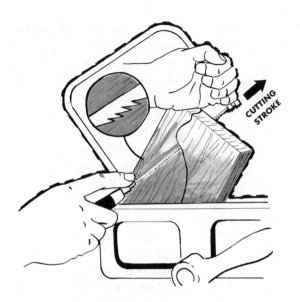

Figure 6-14: Curved cuts in wood can be made with a coping saw. The coping saw has a thin blade and a handle designed to let the blade follow the curve of the cut.

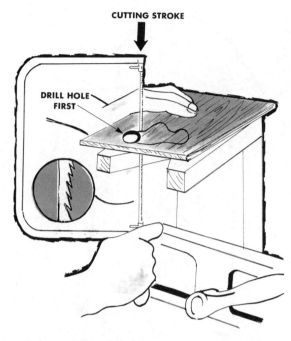

Figure 6-15: After drilling a hole through the wood, the coping saw blade is inserted through the hole and attached to the handle. Depending on the need, the blade may also be turned to cut on either the forward or backward stroke.

SELF CHECK

1. List the three handsaws used for straight cuts.
2. What does a ripsaw do?
3. How wide is the kerf?
4. What does a miter box do?

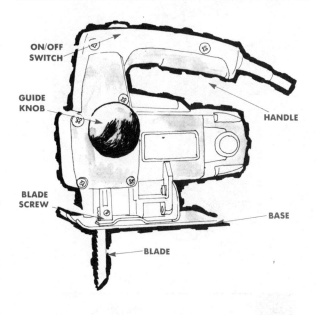

ON/OFF
SWITCH

GUIDE
KNOB

HANDLE

BLADE
SCREW

BASE

BLADE

Figure 7-1: The portable saber saw is also sometimes called a bayonet saw. It is used for cutting straight lines and curves.

Saber saws (figure 7-1) are electric handsaws that are used to cut straight lines and curves. The saber saw has a blade similar to a coping saw blade. However, it is heavier, and it cuts on the up-stroke of its up and down action. By placing the work to be cut face down, the splintering caused by the blade will be on the back surface.

Like all power equipment, the saber saw must be treated with respect. Before using a saber saw, the operator must know its safety rules (figure 7-2).

All cuts, straight or curved, are always made on the waste side of the line (figure 7-3). Guides and attachments are available for cutting straight lines and circles (figures 7-3 and 7-4). However, most woodworkers practice until they can follow any line freehand.

●DISCONNECT THE PLUG WHEN CHANGING BLADES AND WHENEVER YOU ARE THROUGH USING THE TOOL.

●BE SURE THE ELECTRICAL CORD IS NOT FRAYED AND IS SUITABLY GROUNDED.

●CLAMP THE WORK SECURELY.

●NEVER FORCE THE TOOL FASTER THAN IT CAN CUT.

●USE THE RIGHT BLADE OR CUTTER FOR THE JOB.

●CARRY THE TOOL BY THE HANDLE, NOT THE CORD.

●WEAR EYE PROTECTION.

Figure 7-2: Safety rules for the power saber saw and other power equipment.

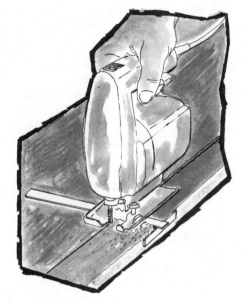

Figure 7-3: The saber saw is adjusted so that the kerf is on the waste side of the line.

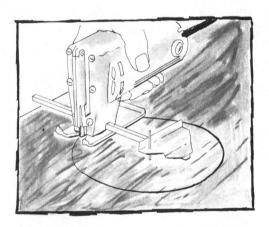

Figure 7-4: The saber saw has an attachment that will ensure the cutting of a perfect circle.

SELF CHECK

1. In what direction does a saber saw blade cut?
2. Which side of the work faces up?
3. What is the waste side of the line?
4. Why is eye protection necessary when operating a saber saw?

The <u>jigsaw</u> (figure 8-1) is also called the scroll saw. It is used for cutting curves and openings in thin wood (figures 8-2 and 8-3). Because it is easy to use on complicated curves, the jigsaw can be fun. Certain safety precautions must be observed (figure 8-4).

Like a saber saw, the jigsaw blade moves up and down. It cuts on the downstroke so the stock should face up to avoid splintering.

Wide blades with fewer teeth are used for large curves in thicker wood. Narrow, fine-toothed blades are best for sharp curves and thinner material.

Note that the lower chuck should be at its highest point when you are changing blades.

To follow a line, adjust the hold-down to the stock thickness, and start the cut on the waste side of the line. Without cutting into the line, slowly feed and turn the work so the blade follows the line (figure 8-5). If the blade starts toward the line, leave the saw running but stop feeding the stock forward. Turn the stock until the blade is back on the path.

Complex cuts should be planned before starting to cut. Mentally break

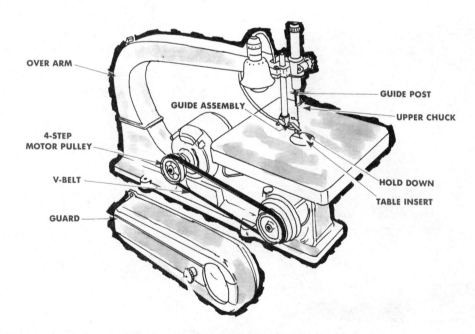

Figure 8-1: The jigsaw is also called the scroll saw. The blade moves up and down and cuts only on the downstroke. Splintering caused by the blade occurs on the underside of the stock being cut.

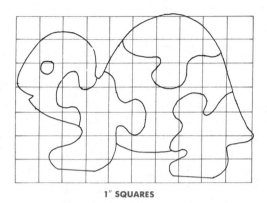

1″ SQUARES

Figure 8-2: Complicated cuts such as these puzzles are made possible with the jigsaw. The jigsaw easily follows intricate curves in thin wood, leaving a narrow kerf and a relatively finished cut in the wood.

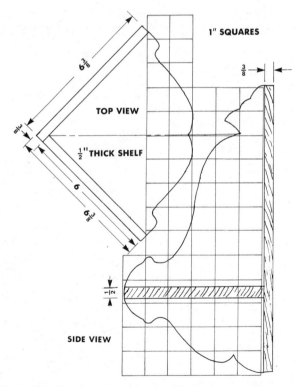

1″ SQUARES

TOP VIEW

½″ THICK SHELF

SIDE VIEW

Figure 8-3: Note that the pattern for this corner wall shelf only shows one side. The same pattern is used to make the other side piece with the addition of the thickness of the wood to one side.

●ADJUST THE JIG SAW ONLY WHEN THE POWER IS OFF.

●HOLD DOWNS SHOULD BE ADJUSTED TO STOCK THICKNESS.

●DO NOT CUT TOO THICK A PIECE OF STOCK.

●WEAR EYE PROTECTION.

●FEED THE WORK SLOWLY TO THE BLADE.

Figure 8-4: Safety rules for the jigsaw.

Figure 8-5: Good cuts are made by slowly feeding and turning the work so the blade follows the line on the waste side.

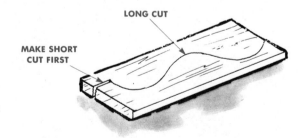

Figure 8-6: Most work has long and short cuts in it. The best place to start is with a short cut when there is a choice between beginning with a long or short cut.

complicated curves into a series of easier cuts. Make short, straight cuts first (figure 8-6). Difficult corners and com-

Figure 8-7: Where the corners are too sharp for an inside curve, they must be roughed out. Then the corner may be cut out from another direction later.

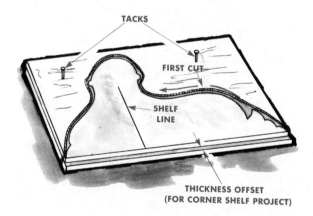

Figure 8-8: When cutting two identical pieces from one pattern, cut them as one piece. In this illustration the pattern in figure 8-3 is laid out on the top board. The second board is offset by its own thickness because this is where the two pieces join. The two are nailed or screwed together on the line that will be covered by the shelf after assembly. Then both pieces are cut as one on the jigsaw. After cutting, the two pieces may be left fastened while the edges are sanded.

plex cuts can be roughed out first (figure 8-7). After the excess wood is gone, smaller cuts can be made closer to the line from different angles.

Stack cutting (figure 8-8) is a good way to make two pieces exactly the same. Simply nail them together and saw them both as one piece. Drive the nails through waste wood areas.

Sawing inside openings with a jigsaw is done the same way as internal cutting is done with a coping saw. Pass a blade through a drill hole in the wood (figure 8-9). Install the blade in the jigsaw and make the cut (figure 8-10).

Figure 8-10: Once the blade is attached to the jigsaw, the cut is started through the waste wood. The kerf is kept on the waste side of the line.

SELF CHECK

1. Which work surface faces up on the jigsaw?
2. What blade is used for thick stock?
3. What kind of cutting are fine-toothed blades used for?
4. How is an internal cut made with a jigsaw?

Figure 8-9: Sawing inside openings with the jigsaw is done the same way as internal cutting with a coping saw. A blade is passed through a hole drilled in the waste area of the work. Then the piece is cut on the jigsaw.

The <u>band saw</u> (figure 9-1) is used to make freehand, irregular cuts like the jigsaw. But it will do it faster and in thicker material. Although faster and stronger than the jigsaw, the band saw has some drawbacks:

● Jigsaw cuts have smoother surfaces than band saw cuts

● Band saw blades are too wide to make sharp curves

● It takes more skill to operate the high speed band saw

Cutting on a band saw is done by an <u>endless blade</u> driven on large wheels at the top and bottom of the machine. Band saws are described by wheel diameter. Fourteen inch band saws are a common size.

The band saw blade is constantly moving downward through the table (figure 9-2). This is the cutting stroke. Its cutting speed makes the band saw more dangerous than the jigsaw and proper safety precautions should always be observed (figure 9-3).

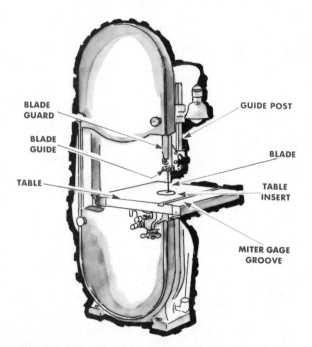

Figure 9-1: Band saws make freehand, irregular cuts like the jigsaw. The difference is the band saw has a continuous blade which cuts in a downward direction.

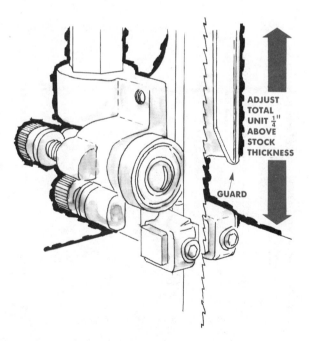

Figure 9-2: The band saw has a heavy, flexible blade which is driven on large wheels above and below the cutting table.

- DRESS RIGHT, WEAR EYE PROTECTION, TUCK IN LOOSE CLOTHING AND HAIR.

- ADJUST THE UPPER BLADE GUIDE ABOUT $\frac{1}{4}$ INCH ABOVE THE STOCK. NEVER CUT WITH MORE BLADE EXPOSED THAN NECESSARY.

- DO NOT CUT ROUND STOCK (LIKE DOWELS).

- FEED STOCK SLOWLY.

- DO NOT TURN SO SHARPLY THAT THE BLADE TWISTS.

- AVOID BACKING UP. IF NECESSARY TO BACK OUT OF A LONG CURVE, TURN THE POWER OFF. WHEN THE BLADE STOPS, CAREFULLY BACK THE WORK OUT WITH OUT KINKING THE BLADE.

- NEVER HOLD THE WORK WITH YOUR HANDS DIRECTLY IN LINE WITH THE BLADE.

- ALWAYS KEEP HANDS AT LEAST THREE INCHES AWAY FROM THE BLADE.

- SHUT OFF THE POWER IF YOU HEAR ANY UNUSUAL NOISE. (CLICKING SOUNDS INDICATE A CRACKED BLADE.)

- USE ONLY SHARP BLADES. DULL BLADES REQUIRE EXTRA FEEDING PRESSURE. YOUR HAND MAY SLIP INTO THE BLADE WHEN THE WORK IS SUDDENLY FREED AT THE END OF THE CUT.

Figure 9-3: Band saws are dangerous and require extra safety precautions.

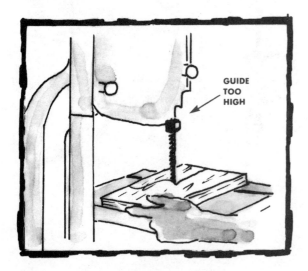

GUIDE TOO HIGH

Figure 9-4: Hand protection starts by keeping your hands away from the blade. Having the guide and shield up too high is dangerous.

Basic sawing is done by standing to the left of the band saw table. The right hand feeds the work and the left hand guides it from the side. Left handed people should stand on the right side and feed with their left hand. The feed hand is kept far from the blade (figure 9-4). Cuts are made on the waste side of line (figure 9-5) and complex cuts are made after roughing (figures 9-6 and 9-7).

Relief cuts are short cuts that are made straight into the layout line. They make sharp outside curves possible despite the wide band saw blade (figure 9-8).

A ripping fence is a straight guide on a saw. Straight line sawing can be

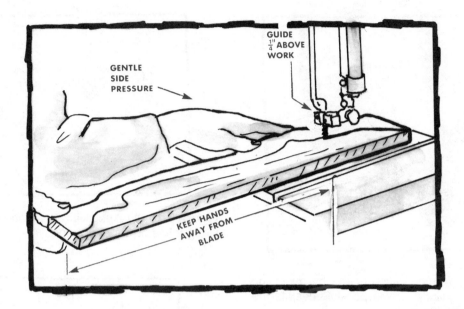

Figure 9-5: With the blade shield down to within 1/4 inch of the work, cutting on the band saw is much safer.

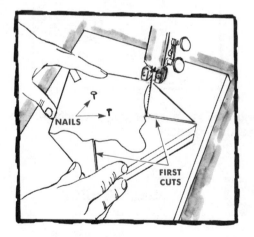

Figure 9-6: Make relief cuts first, then second cuts will be easier.

Figure 9-7: "Nibble" cuts make narrow grooves. Move the blade in and out with short strokes.

done on a band saw if it has a fence. If it doesn't, a straight piece of wood may be clamped to the saw table to be used as a ripping fence (figure 9-9). Im-

provised equipment such as this ripping fence must always be approved by the instructor before you use it.

Skilled operators can saw straight

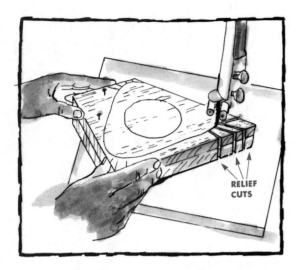

Figure 9-8: Relief cuts straight into the layout line make sharp outside curves possible despite the wide band saw blade.

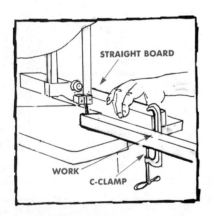

Figure 9-9: A piece of wood may be clamped to the band saw table and used as a ripping fence.

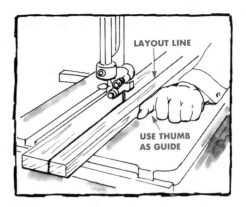

Figure 9-10: It takes skill with a band saw to saw straight lines without a guide.

Figure 9-11: A miter gage attachment makes crosscutting easier.

lines freehand (figure 9-10). Crosscutting can also be done freehand. But some band saw tables have a slot for a <u>miter gage</u> attachment with makes crosscutting easier (figure 9-11).

SELF CHECK

1. When is a jigsaw better than a band saw?
2. How is the size of a band saw described?
3. Why is a relief cut used?
4. What cut does the miter gage attachment make easier?

For a skilled woodworker the band saw can do many special jobs. Even though the technique may not be ordinary, the operator must still apply all the usual safety rules to the work.

The most common special cuts that are made on a band saw are:

● Bevel ripping
● Resawing
● Slice ripping
● Compound band sawing

Bevel ripping (figure 10-1) is done with the table tilted to the desired angle. A fence is a handy guide for feeding the work.

Resawing reduces the thickness of the wood (figure 10-2). A pivot block is a better guide than a fence in resawing. The blade tends to lead (follow) the grain of the wood. With the pivot block, this leading can be corrected by changing the feed direction. Always use a push stick when you are finishing the cut (figure 10-3).

Slice ripping is a good way to make identical pieces. First the solid wood is

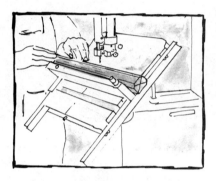

Figure 10-1: Bevel ripping is done with the table tilted to the desired angle.

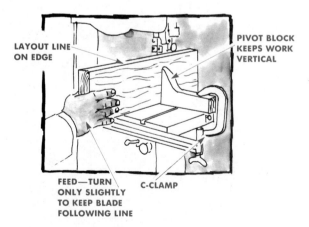

LAYOUT LINE ON EDGE

PIVOT BLOCK KEEPS WORK VERTICAL

FEED—TURN ONLY SLIGHTLY TO KEEP BLADE FOLLOWING LINE

C-CLAMP

Figure 10-2: In resawing (cutting stock to a new thickness) the blade will follow the grain of the wood unless the operator is careful.

PUSH STICK

Figure 10-3: A push stick is a good safety precaution in resawing.

cut to shape on the band saw (figure 10-4). Then it is ripped into thinner, identical pieces (figure 10-5). A simple jig is often used with slice ripping. The shingle jig shown in figure 10-8 is a good example. It is used to slice rip the shingles for the birdhouse project in figures 10-6 through 10-9.

Figure 10-4: Slice ripping is a two-step process. First the thick piece is cut like any other piece of work.

Figure 10-6: When evaluating a project, like this birdhouse, it is important to think about the best and easiest way to cut the parts.

Figure 10-5: The second step in slice ripping is to slice off identical pieces from the cut work.

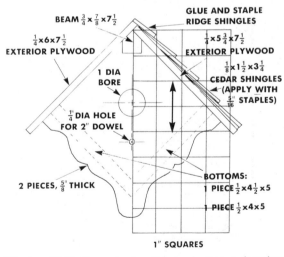

Figure 10-7: By reducing the project to a drawing of its parts it becomes possible to imagine how to make each part.

Compound band sawing is a way of getting good cuts on the band saw when making unusual four-sided shapes like the candle holder shown in

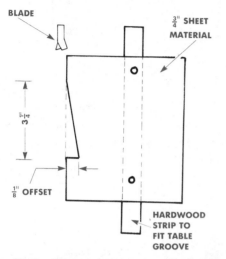

Figure 10-8: Obviously shingles can be slice ripped. This is done by using a tapered shingle cutting jig, and turning the stock end-to-end for each cut.

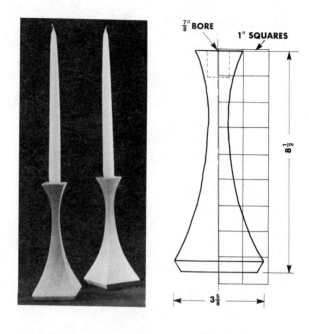

Figure 10-10: Compound band sawing is necessary to make unusual 4-sided shapes.

Figure 10-9: Because cedar and redwood are good outside woods, shingles are rip sliced from a 2 inch piece of a scrap cedar or redwood.

Figure 10-11: The template pattern is drawn on two sides of the wood block using a half template.

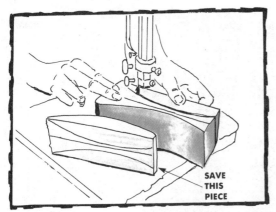

Figure 10-12: Using the band saw, one side of the block is cut to the pattern.

Figure 10-13: Turn the block and make the second set of cuts.

figure 10-10. The stock is squared so it is equal in thickness and width, and has right angle corners. Then the pattern is laid on one face and edge (figure 10-11). The pattern is cut as usual (figure 10-12). Then the pieces are nailed back onto the block, keeping the nails in a waste area. The block is turned, the pattern drawn again, and cut. By rebuilding the block each time, identical cuts are possible on all four sides (figure 10-13).

SELF CHECK

1. How is bevel ripping done?
2. What is resawing?
3. How is a push stick used?
4. What happens when a blade leads in resawing?

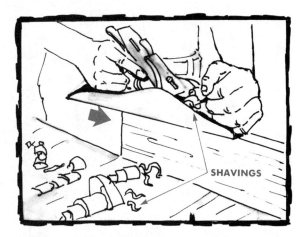

Figure 11-1: Hand planes cut by removing thin shavings from the wood.

Figure 11-2: Most planes look very much alike. This is a jack plane, one of the most commonly used planes.

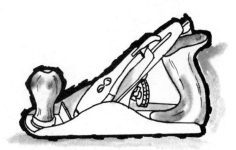

Figure 11-3: Note the smooth plane is shorter than the jack plane.

Hand planes cut wood by removing thin shavings (figure 11-1). Two common woodworking planes are the jack plane (figure 11-2) and the smooth plane (figure 11-3). Except for length, most planes are similar to each other.

Basically hand planes are used to smooth or true (make a surface flat) rough sawn surfaces. How well the plane works depends on the blade.

A properly sharpened and adjusted plane is essential to good work. To protect the blade and its adjustment the plane is always laid on its side when not in use.

It takes practice to properly sharpen and adjust a plane blade. The plane comes apart by removing the lever cap (figure 11-4). Next to come off are the plane iron and plane iron cap. The lever cap can then be used as a screwdriver to tighten and loosen the cap iron screw (figure 11-5).

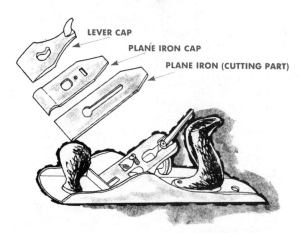

Figure 11-4: The first step in taking a plane apart is to remove the lever cap.

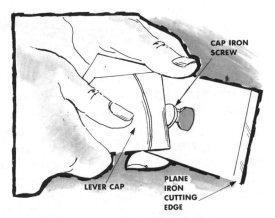

Figure 11-5: Using the lever cap as a screw-driver, the cap iron screw is loosened.

Figure 11-8: By sighting along the bottom, the adjusting lever and nut are adjusted to obtain an even shaving for the thickness of the cut.

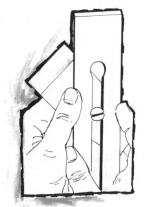

Figure 11-6: The iron cap is taken off so the blade may be sharpened.

Figure 11-9: To plane an edge, the plane must be held square to the stock face.

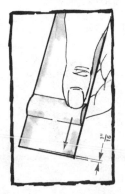
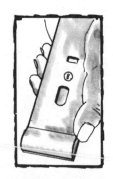
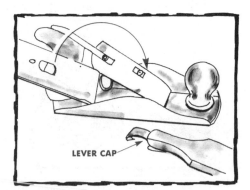

Figure 11-7: To reassemble the plane, the plane iron cap is moved forward. The screw is tightened. Then the plane iron is inserted and the lever cap and lock put back on.

Figure 11-10: Surfaces are planed to face rough lumber or reduce thickness.

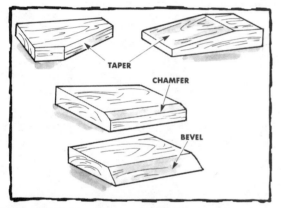

Figure 11-11: Common finishing cuts with a hand plane are the taper, chamfer, and bevel.

Sharpening is necessary if the cutting edge is nicked or shiny. The cap iron must be removed before sharpening (figure 11-6). A sharp edge does not reflect light. After the edge is sharpened, the plane is reassembled (figure 11-7). The plane is then adjusted for an even cut (figure 11-8).

Once the plane is sharpened and properly adjusted, it may be used in four ways:

- Planing an edge (figure 11-9), which is always done with the grain.
- Planing a surface (figure 11-10), usually to face rough lumber or reduce thickness
- Planing bevels, chamfers, and tapers (figure 11-11).
- Planing end grain (figure 11-12), best done with a block plane.

SELF CHECK

1. Name the two most common planes.
2. How is a plane taken apart?
3. When does a blade need sharpening?
4. What is a block plane used for?

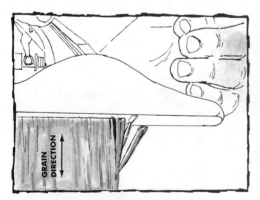

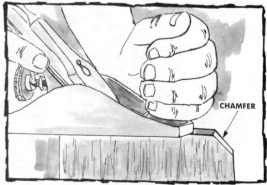

Figure 11-12: Planing clear across the end grain even with a block plane will cause splintering. A chamfer cut will allow planing without splintering.

The block plane (figure 12-1) is a special type of hand plane. It is very small and easily used with one hand. The block plane has a low cutting angle. Unlike the smooth and jack planes, the plane iron is installed with its cutting bevel up.

This plane is easier to control than other planes. It is designed for planing end grain (figure 12-2). The block plane is ideal for planing doors or drawers (figure 12-3) to fit. It is also used to cut bevels (figure 12-4) and chamfers (figure 12-5). As with any type of plane, always try to work with the grain.

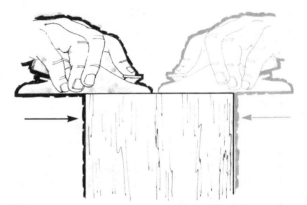

Figure 12-2: The block plane is designed for planing end grains.

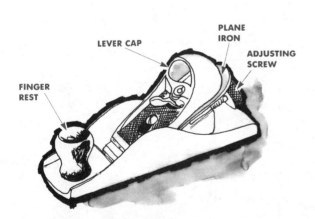

Figure 12-1: The block plane is very small and easily used with one hand.

PLANE IRON

LEVER CAP

ADJUSTING SCREW

FINGER REST

Figure 12-3: Sticking drawers are cured by planing with the block plane.

Figure 12-4: Bevels are easily cut with the block plane.

Figure 12-5: Besides cutting chamfers, the block plane may also be used for taking corners off plywood.

SELF CHECK

1. Why is the block plane special?
2. Why is the block plane smaller than the jack plane?
3. What is different about the block plane iron cutting bevel?
4. What is the block plane's ideal use?

The woodworker uses two terms for the operation of putting holes in wood (figure 13-1). They are not interchangeable because they have special meanings. The terms are:

● Drilling
● Boring

Drilling usually refers to cutting holes 1/4 inch or smaller in diameter with twist drills. Twist drills come in sizes from 1/32 inch to 1/4 inch. They are used in a tool called a hand drill (figure 13-2). The shank of a twist drill is the same size as the bit. The part that holds the twist drill in the hand drill is called the chuck (figure 13-3).

Boring usually means cutting holes larger than 1/4 inch. The woodworker uses auger bits (figure 13-4), mounted in a tool called a hand brace to bore holes. Auger bits come in sets from 3/16

inch to 1 inch in diameter (figure 13-5). Sizes are marked on the bit tangs in sixteenths of an inch. For example, a bit stamped with the size 6 will make a 3/8 inch diameter hole.

Auger bits are available in sizes larger than 1 inch. But most wood shops use an adjustable bit called an expansive bit (figure 13-6) for boring holes larger than 1 inch.

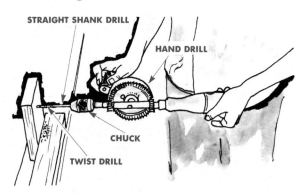

Figure 13-2: Twist drills are used in hand drills. The shank of a twist drill is the same size as the cutting end.

Figure 13-1: When working with wood, small holes are drilled and large holes are bored, as in this flower vase project.

Figure 13-3: The chuck adjusts to the size of the twist drill. When someone describes a hand or power drill as "one-quarter inch" or "three-eighths inch," they mean the largest size the drill chuck will hold.

The <u>hand brace</u> (figure 13-7) has a special chuck which holds the square ended auger bit (figure 13-8).

Boring with a bit and brace begins by locating the center of the hole. The small screw tip will set the bit (figure 13-9). A square is used as a guide to make true vertical holes (figure 13-10). Turning the handle of the brace will force the bit into the wood.

To eliminate splintering when the bit bores clear through the wood (figure 13-11) woodworkers can do one of two things. They may back the auger out when the point of the feed screw breaks all the way through and finish boring the hole out from the backside (figure 13-12). Or they may clamp scrap wood to the wood being bored. When the auger bores all the way through it will splinter the scrap, but not the work piece.

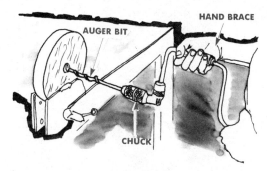

Figure 13-7: The hand brace is built so the woodworker can use more strength to bore a hole than with a hand drill.

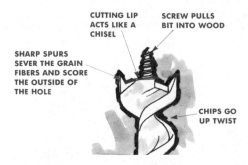

CUTTING LIP ACTS LIKE A CHISEL

SCREW PULLS BIT INTO WOOD

SHARP SPURS SEVER THE GRAIN FIBERS AND SCORE THE OUTSIDE OF THE HOLE

CHIPS GO UP TWIST

Figure 13-4: To bore holes larger than 1/4 inch, woodworkers use the auger bit.

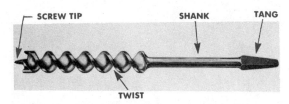

SCREW TIP

SHANK

TANG

TWIST

Figure 13-5: The usual auger bit is 3/16 inch to 1 inch in diameter. Auger bit sizes are always marked in sixteenths of an inch.

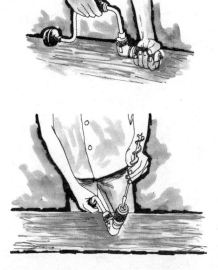

Figure 13-6: Expansive bits are used to bore holes more than 1 inch in diameter.

Figure 13-8: Twist drills may slip around in the chuck when there is too much pressure. Square ended auger bits don't slip in their special chuck.

1. What is the difference between boring and drilling?
2. What is the difference between a hand drill and a brace?
3. What does the chuck do?
4. What is another name for an adjustable auger bit?

Figure 13-11: When the auger bit breaks through a piece of wood, it causes splintering. Where the screw tip comes out is called the exit hole.

SCREW TIP

Figure 13-9: The auger bit is built to avoid slipping. The small screw tip pulls the bit into the wood and keeps it from slipping off center.

SCREW TIP

Figure 13-12: When the feed screw breaks through the lumber being bored, the auger bit can be removed and started once again through the exit hole.

Figure 13-10: Straight holes are made possible by using a try-square as a guide.

Portable electric drills (figure 14-1) are usually called 1/4 inch or 3/8 inch drills. The number means that the

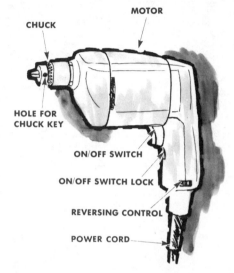

CHUCK

MOTOR

HOLE FOR CHUCK KEY

ON/OFF SWITCH

ON/OFF SWITCH LOCK

REVERSING CONTROL

POWER CORD

Figure 14-1: Most portable electric drills are 1/4 inch or 3/8 inch models. The larger drill will usually have a heavier motor, but not always.

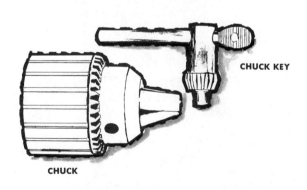

CHUCK KEY

CHUCK

Figure 14-2: The size description of an electric drill is the largest size twist drill the chuck will hold. The chuck key tightens the chuck on the drill bit.

largest twist drill shank diameter the drill chuck will hold is 1/4 or 3/8 inch. Most electric drills have geared chucks that require special chuck keys to open or close them (figure 14-2).

THREE-PRONG GROUNDED PLUG AND RECEPTACLE

Figure 14-3: Many drills have a third, or ground, wire that ends in a prong in the plug. If there should be an accident—like drilling into its own wire—the ground wire will get rid of the electricity that might injure the drill user.

TWO-PRONG PLUGS ARE SAFE ON A DOUBLE INSULATED TOOL

Figure 14-4: Double insulated drills don't need the extra ground wire. They will not transmit electricity to the user of the electric drill.

There are two kinds of electric drills currently on the market:

● Grounded drills
● Double insulated drills

A <u>grounded drill</u> has an electrical plug with three prongs (figure 14-3). The third prong provides protection against electrical shock. If the drill has a short, the current will run out the third prong and into the ground.

<u>Double insulated drills</u> don't need the extra wire and prong. They come with two prong plugs (figure 14-4). They are usually marked "DOUBLE INSULATED" (figure 14-5). The symbol "UL" on electrical equipment means that Underwriter's Laboratory has tested the equipment for safety and approved it.

Portable electric drills may have variable speed controls. They may rotate in either direction (forward or re-

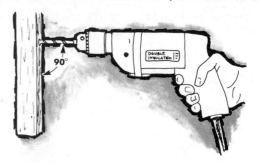

Figure 14-5: Notice how the drill is held square to the work to make a straight hole. Both grounded and double insulated drills use the regular twist drill which is also used in hand drills.

TWIST DRILL

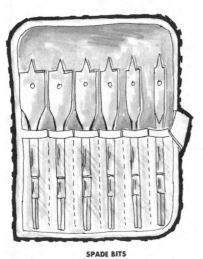

SPADE BITS

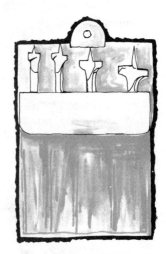

POWER BORE BITS

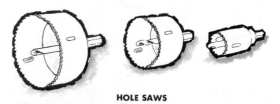

HOLE SAWS

Figure 14-6: Modern electric drills have a variety of special cutting tools and attachments.

verse). Variable speed models can be set up to drive screws or hole saws into wood. Different kinds of cutting tools and bits are made for all electric drills (figure 14-6).

Figure 14-7: A T-bevel is used to line up the bit at the desired angle. A piece of tape may be wound around the drill bit to indicate the depth of the hole.

To use a portable electric drill, center punch the center of the hole with a scratch awl. Place the bit in the dimple made by the awl and start the drill. A square or a T-bevel (figure 14-7), can be used to control the angle.

Jigs (figure 14-8) or collars (figure 14-9) may be used to control the location, angle, or depth of the hole.

SELF CHECK

1. How is the size of a portable electric drill determined?
2. How would you drill two holes the same depth?
3. How would you start drilling a hole?
4. What can be used to guide the angle of a drill hole?

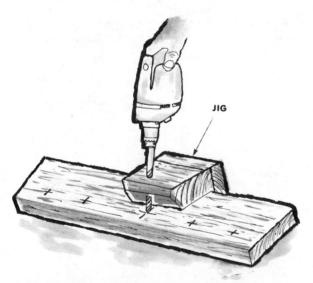

Figure 14-8: Jigs allow the woodworker to drill holes at identical angles and distances from the edge of the wood.

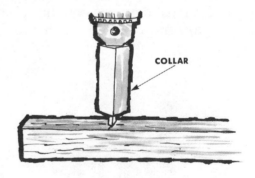

Figure 14-9: One of several ways to control the depth of the hole being drilled.

DRILL PRESS DRILLING AND BORING

The drill press (figure 15-1) makes very accurate holes in wood. Many projects, like the candle holder in figure 15-2, are done more easily with the help of the drill press. With the right attachments the drill press can also be used to sand and shape.

Drill presses are made in fourteen, fifteen and seventeen inch sizes. A fourteen inch drill press can be used to drill a hole in the center of a fourteen inch wide board. This means that the center of the chuck is only seven inches from the column. Chucks on drill presses usually have a one-half inch diameter capacity.

The number of revolutions the chuck rotates every minute (rpm or revolutions per minute) is called the spindle speed. On most drill presses the spindle speeds vary from three hundred to five

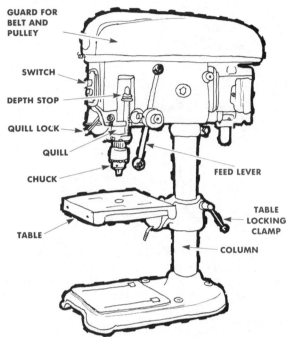

Figure 15-1: The drill press eliminates most of the inaccuracies of hand held drilling tools.

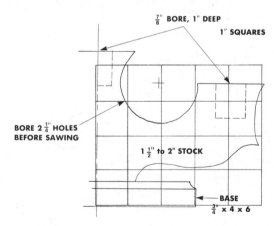

Figure 15-2: Although it takes practice to bore big holes straight with a hand drill or brace, the drill press makes such work easy.

- WEAR EYE PROTECTION, TUCK IN LOOSE CLOTHING AND HAIR, BUTTON SLEEVES OR ROLL THEM ABOVE ELBOWS.
- BE SURE THE SPEED IS RIGHT.
- TIGHTEN BITS FIRMLY WITH THE CHUCK KEY.
- REMOVE THE CHUCK KEY!
- CLAMP SMALL PIECES TO THE TABLE.
- ALSO CLAMP WORK WHEN BORING IN KNOTTY WOOD AND WHEN MAKING LARGE HOLES.
- USE A FLAT SCRAP BOARD UNDER YOUR WORK WHEN DRILLING CLEAR THROUGH THE WOOD.

Figure 15-3: These safety rules for the drill press should be used at all times.

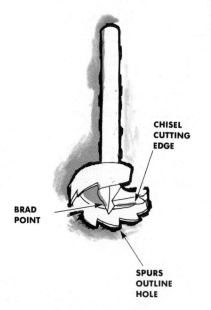

Figure 15-4: Multi-spur bits cut very clean holes.

Figure 15-5: The forstner bit is guided by its rim and has no extending center point. It makes clean holes with flat bottoms.

er the bit size, the faster the speed. Use slow speeds when making large holes.

A drill press is a safe machine to use if safety rules are observed (figure 15-3).

Machine boring tools include those used in portable electric drills. Two other drill press tools that cut slick, clean holes are the multi-spur bit (figure 15-4) and the forstner bit (figure 15-5).

Boring holes to a specific depth (figure 15-6) is easily done by setting the depth stop. When set, this adjustment limits the vertical feed.

thousand RPM. Speed is changed on most drill presses by shifting a V-belt on a set of pulleys or with a variable speed control. Different jobs require different speeds. In general, the small-

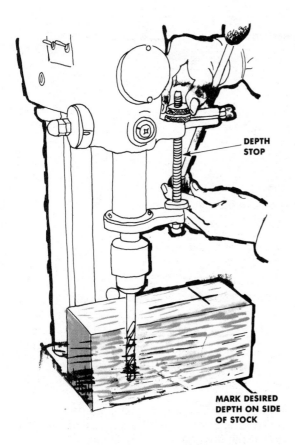

DEPTH
STOP

MARK DESIRED
DEPTH ON SIDE
OF STOCK

Figure 15-6: An aid on the drill press is the depth stop. By setting it before boring, the drill stops at a certain depth.

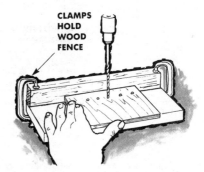

CLAMPS
HOLD
WOOD
FENCE

Figure 15-7: Drilling holes in a perfectly straight row can be done by clamping a wood fence to the table.

SELF CHECK

1. What is the size capacity of most drill press chucks?
2. What does rpm mean?
3. Should large holes be cut at fast or slow speeds?
4. Why must the chuck key must be removed from the chuck before turning on the power?

Boring with the aid of a <u>fence</u> (figure 15-7) is useful for assuring that each hole will be exactly the same distance from the edge of a board.

Chisels are used to smooth surfaces, shape wood, and make parts fit together (figure 16-1). Wood chisels are of two types:
- Tang
- Socket

Tang chisels (figure 16-2) have part of the blade extending into the handle. Socket chisels (figure 16-3) have a cone-shaped part into which the wood or plastic handle fits.

Chisels are sized by the width of the cutting blade. A typical chisel set includes 1/4, 1/2, 3/4, and 1 inch sizes.

Dull chisels cause poor quality work and are dangerous. For heavy cuts a wood mallet is used to drive the chisel (figure 16-4). Deep rough cuts are made bevel side down (figure 16-5). The bevel side is up for a fine cut (figure 16-6).

Gouges (figure 16-7) are like chisels except they have curved cutting edges. The insides of free form bowls and trays are hand carved with gouges (figure 16-8). They are used in much the same way as chisels.

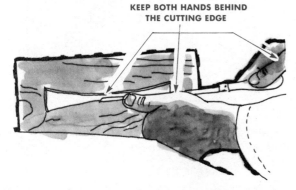

Figure 16-1: Chisels are used like this to smooth a cut surface. Note how the bevel is up and the work is securely held in a vise.

Figure 16-2: Tang chisels have an end that fits into the wood handle.

Figure 16-3: Socket chisels have the handle fit into themselves.

Figure 16-4: Heavy cuts are made with a chisel and a wood mallet. The cutting bevel faces down.

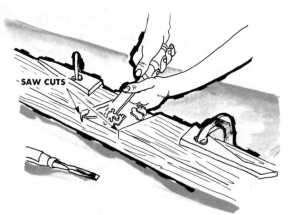

Figure 16-5: Lap joints can be cut with a chisel. Notice saw cuts made to sever the grain fibers.

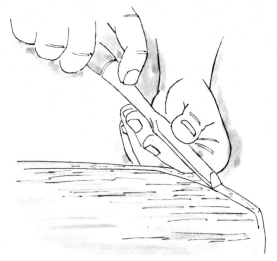

Figure 16-6: Finishing cuts are made with the bevel up.

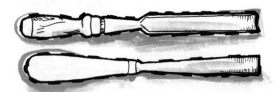

Figure 16-7: Gouges have curved cutting edges. They come in both tang and socket varieties.

Figure 16-8: Gouges are used to follow the contour of curved surfaces such as hollowing out a free form bowl.

SELF CHECK

1. What are the two types of chisels?
2. Should a chisel be used bevel side up or down when making fine cuts?
3. What are the three types of chisels used for?
4. How are gouges similar to chisels?

SINGLE-CUT

Figure 17-1: The single cut file is used on metal and for fine finishing of hard woods.

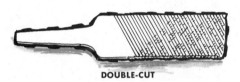

DOUBLE-CUT

Figure 17-2: Double cut files are coarser. They remove more material but leave a rougher surface than the single cut file.

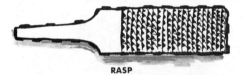

RASP

Figure 17-3: Rasps have large triangular teeth that are used for coarse, rough work. Rasps cut faster than files, but they make rough cuts that must be smoothed later.

Figure 17-4: Because ground off waste can't build up around their teeth, forming tools may be more efficient than regular files which need frequent cleaning.

Filing and rasping are methods of smoothing or shaping wood after it has been rough cut. The three most common tools used in this work are:
● Files
● Rasps
● Forming tools

Files are metal bars with teeth cut on their surfaces. The single cut file (figure 17-1) is used on metal and for fine finishing of hard woods. Double cut files (figure 17-2) are much coarser than single cut files.

Rasps (figure 17-3) are very coarse files. They cut fast but leave a rough surface.

Forming tools (figure 17-4) are thin blades of steel mounted on a holder. The blades have many individual sharp teeth. A hole behind each tooth prevents clogging as happens with normal files and rasps.

Files, rasps, and forming tools are ideal for shaping curved surfaces (figure 17-5). All work should be clamped down, and a handle must be fitted on the tang before using a file (figure 17-6). This protects the worker's hands.

The most common types of woodworking files are the flat file, the half-round file, and the round or "rat tail" file (figure 17-7).

The teeth of a woodworking file clog very easily. They are cleaned with a file card (figure 17-8). Hold the handle of the file in one hand and the file card

Figure 17-5: Files, rasps, or forming tools are needed to form curved surfaces.

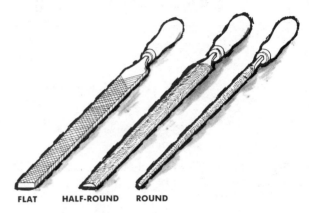

Figure 17-7: Common woodworking files are the flat file, half-round file, and round or "rat tail" file.

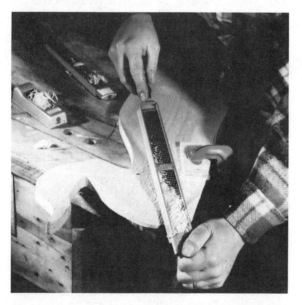

Figure 17-6: Two important safety precautions are to keep work being filed clamped down and always use a handle on the file.

in the other. Clean the file by brushing the file card over the file in the direction the teeth are cut.

Figure 17-8: A file card is a special brush used to keep the teeth of a file clean.

SELF CHECK

1. What are three kinds of file teeth?
2. How is a rasp different from a file?
3. Name the three most commonly used woodworking files.
4. Why are handles put on files before they are used?

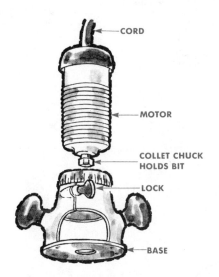

Figure 18-1: The portable electric router has only two major parts, the motor and base.

The portable electric router (figure 18-1) is so useful to woodworkers that many call it a portable workshop. Two of its handiest uses are making:

● Decorative edges on boards
● Joint fitting cuts

The two parts of the router are the motor and base. The cutting bit is spun at between twenty and thirty thousand rpm by the motor. This high speed cuts surfaces so smooth that little sanding is needed. Hundreds of different router bit designs and sizes offer a great selection of cuts.

Decorative edges on boards (figure 18-2) can be done easily by the beginner. Irregular or curved edges are shaped as simply as straight edges.

Joint fitting cuts like rabbets, grooves, and dadoes (figure 18-3) are also cut cleanly and quickly with a router. Many cuts are done with special bits, but the standard bit alone is adequate for good dadoes and rabbets (figure 18-4).

Any sharp tool which operates at the speeds a router does can be dangerous. All safety precautions must be observed when you are operating a router (figure 18-5).

To change the bit, unplug and remove the motor from the guide (figure 18-6). The threaded collet nut (figure 18-7) is loosened. The bit is inserted into the collet, then backed out 1/8 inch. With the motor unit on the bench, the collet is tightened with the wrenches.

The motor is put in the base (figure 18-8) with the lock nut loose. When the bit sticks through the base to the desired depth of cut (figure 18-9) the lock is tightened.

Edge forming (figure 18-10) is done with the router base flat on the surface of the work. By feeding from left to right while facing the work, the cut is against the rotation of the bit. Make shallow cuts. Then cut again deeper in the same groove.

The feed should be steady. Stopping the router movement with the bit spinning will burn the wood.

Groove forming cuts (figure 18-11) are made easier by clamping a

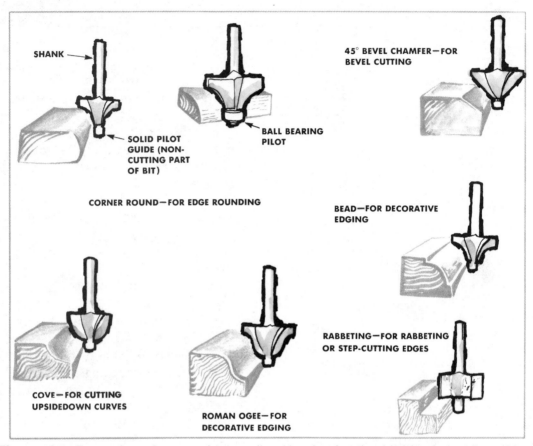

Figure 18-2: Decorative edges are done easily with edge forming bits that have pilot guides.

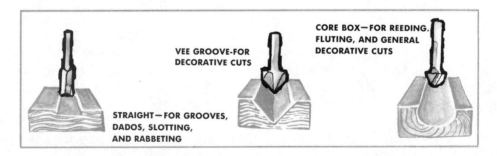

Figure 18-3: Basic joint fitting cuts such as rabbets, dadoes, and grooves can be done with router bits that do not have pilot guides.

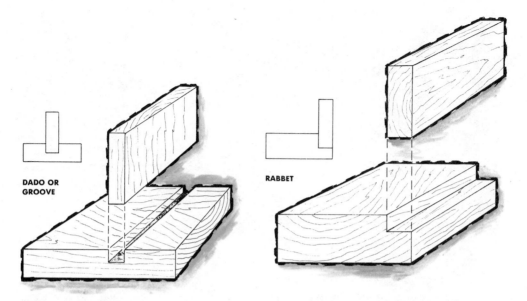

DADO OR
GROOVE

RABBET

Figure 18-4: The straight cutting bit on a router cuts good dadoes and rabbets.

●BE SURE THE TOOL IS PROPERLY GROUNDED.

●CLAMP WORK FIRMLY.

●DRESS RIGHT! WEAR GOGGLES, NO LOOSE HAIR OR CLOTHING.

●DISCONNECT PLUG WHEN MAKING ADJUSTMENTS OR CHANGING BITS.

●KEEP BOTH HANDS ON KNOBS (OR HANDLE).

●ALLOW THE ROUTER TO REACH FULL SPEED BEFORE ADVANCING IT INTO THE
   WORK.

Figure 18-5: Safety precautions for the router are important just as they are for any other high speed cutting machines.

Figure 18-6: To change the bit, the router is taken apart.

Figure 18-7: Some routers have a little finger lock so the collet nut can be loosened with one wrench. Other routers require the use of two wrenches for the same job.

Figure 18-8: The motor is returned to the base. The lock is not tightened until the router bit depth is properly set.

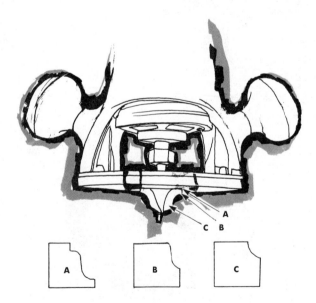

Figure 18-9: Depth of cut is measured as the distance from the router base to the tip of the router blade.

Figure 18-10: Edge forming is done with the router base flat on the surface of the work.

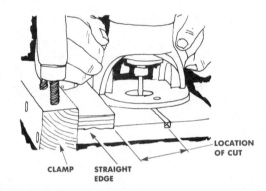

CLAMP   STRAIGHT EDGE   LOCATION OF CUT

Figure 18-11: A straight groove can be cut by using a straight edge as a guide against the router base.

straight-edge to the top of the surface to be cut. A straight groove is guaranteed using the straightedge as a guide against the router base.

SELF CHECK

1. Is it easier to shape curved edges than it is to cut straight edges?
2. What are the two parts of the router?
3. What safety precautions are necessary when routing?
4. How is a deep cut made?

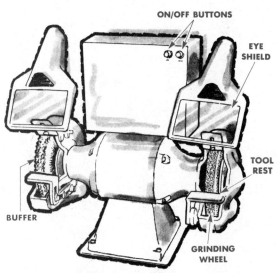

Figure 19-1: Grinders usually have two wheels of different textures. Sometimes one end of the shaft will be a grinder while the other end is a buffer.

To the skilled woodworker, nothing is worse than trying to use a dull tool. Skillful woodworkers must master these edge tool sharpening jobs:

● Grinding—the shaping of a new bevel
● Honing—the "tune-up" of an existing edge

Grinders (figure 19-1) have two round grinding wheels, one at each end of the motor shaft. The wheels are made of abrasive grains glued together in round wheel shapes. Grinding wheels may be made of coarse, medium, or fine abrasives. Some safety concerns for using the grinder are given in figure 19-2.

● WEAR EYE PROTECTION.

● KEEP TOOL REST TIGHT AND NOT MORE THAN 1/8" FROM THE WHEEL.

● GRIND ON THE FACE OF THE WHEEL. THAT IS THE PART OF THE WHEEL "FACING" YOU AS THE OPERATOR.

● DO NOT GRIND ON THE SIDE OF THE WHEEL WITHOUT INSTRUCTOR'S CLOSE SUPERVISION.

Figure 19-2: Although grinders are not sharp-edged cutting tools, safety precautions must be taken in their operation.

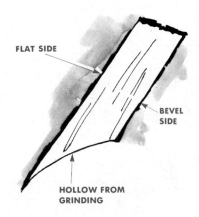

Figure 19-3: When grinding chisels the grinding is always done on the bevel edge.

Tools with nicked edges or worn bevels need regrinding.

On a properly ground bevel, the flat side of the chisel is flat all the way to the edge (figure 19-3). The chisel is ground only on the bevel side. Figure 19-4 shows the bevel length suitable for wood chisels and plane irons. The bevel is about 25°. Some grinders have attachments (figure 19-5) to make holding and grinding the tool easy.

Freehand grinding requires more skill (figure 19-6). The grinder operator uses his or her fingers as a guide along the lower edge of the tool rest. Grinding with very light cuts avoids burning the cutting edge. Cool the tool often in water. Check the edge for squareness with a try-square. Continue grinding until a burr forms on the flat side (figure 19-7). Do not grind the flat side to remove the burr.

Figure 19-5: Attachments can be used to keep the right angle on tools being ground.

Figure 19-6: Freehand grinding requires care. A good tool can be ruined by improper shaping on the grinder.

Figure 19-4: The bevel length suitable for wood chisels and plane irons is shown in this illustration.

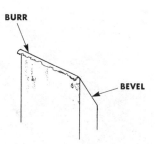

Figure 19-7: Grinding forms a burr on the flat side of the chisel.

Figure 19-8(A): Dull edges require honing, not grinding.

Figure 19-8(B): When hollow grinding has been honed away, the bevel needs regrinding.

Figure 19-9: Hone with the bevel flat on the oil stone. Apply a few drops of oil, and move the tool in a circular motion.

<u>Honing</u> is done with a fine grit oil-stone. Honing between grindings keeps a sharp edge on tools (figure 19-8). A dull edge reflects light, a sharp edge does not.

To hone, apply a few drops of light oil to the whet stone. Place the bevel flat on the surface (figure 19-9). Move the tool with a circular motion working it over the entire surface of the stone. Turn the chisel (or plane iron) over. Hold the flat side of the tool flat to the surface of the stone (figure 19-10). Work the flat side over the stone in the same manner. Alternate honing the back and bevel until the burr is removed. Test for sharpness on a piece of wood.

Boring tools that have spurs and chisel-like cutting lips are sharpened in much the same way. Small single

Figure 19-10: When honing off the burr on the flat side of the chisel, keep the whole flat surface on the stone.

FILE SPUR ON INSIDE ONLY

Figure 19-11: Spurs of all boring tools are filed only on the inside.

Figure 19-12: Use a small single cut file to sharpen spurs and cutter bevels. Never file the spurs on the outside.

cut files are used to resharpen spurs and cutter bevels (figure 19-11 and 19-12). A rule to remember when sharpening auger bits is to never file spurs on the outside. This reduces the clearance of the bit in the hole and it will not cut easily or clean.

Twist drills, handsaws, band saw blades, and router bits are best sharpened with special and expensive equipment. Even skilled woodworkers send these tools to professional tool sharpeners who have the necessary equipment.

SELF CHECK

1. When should a new bevel be ground?
2. Is grinding necessary to make an edge sharper?
3. What is the bevel angle for hand planes and plane irons?
4. How can you tell if an edge is dull just by looking at it?

SMOOTHING

3

The quality of any finely crafted project is reflected in the woodworker's ability to sand or "smooth" it. Flat surfaces should be smooth and slick. Curved surfaces should flow evenly.

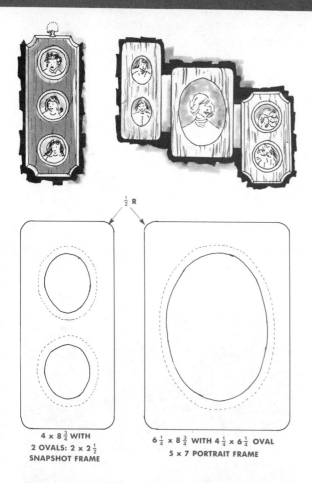

$\frac{1}{2}$ R

4 x 8$\frac{3}{4}$ WITH
2 OVALS: 2 x 2$\frac{1}{2}$
SNAPSHOT FRAME

6$\frac{1}{4}$ x 8$\frac{3}{4}$ WITH 4$\frac{1}{4}$ x 6$\frac{1}{4}$ OVAL
5 x 7 PORTRAIT FRAME

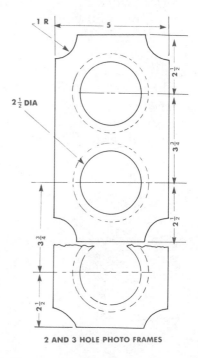

1 R   5

2$\frac{1}{2}$ DIA

2$\frac{1}{2}$

3$\frac{3}{4}$

2$\frac{1}{2}$

3$\frac{3}{4}$

2$\frac{1}{2}$

2 AND 3 HOLE PHOTO FRAMES

PICTURE FRAMES Shown left to right—two small ovals, large oval, two-hole frame, and three-hole frame. In each project a three-eighths by three-eighths inch rabbet is routed around the opening in the back side. Cut pieces of cardboard to fit. Fit and press to hold the pictures in.

Sandpaper is used to cut and smooth wood (figure 20-1). It is like using a file, only the abrasives, which work like teeth, are much finer than file teeth.

Sandpaper is made by gluing the abrasive material to tough cloth or paper backings. Normally there are two kinds of sandpaper abrasives:

● Natural
● Synthetic

Natural abrasives are flint and garnet. Garnet is the most widely used abrasive in woodworking. It is durable, good for both hand and power sanding, and does not lodge in the wood.

Synthetic abrasives are aluminum oxide and silicon carbide. Very hard, synthetic abrasives last longer than garnet does.

Abrasive grains (figure 20-2) are made in different sizes. The size of the

Figure 20-1: Sandpaper is called a coated abrasive because tiny, sharp grains of material are coated on a paper backing.

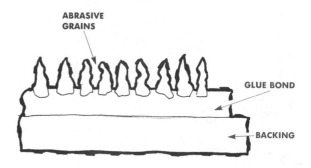

Figure 20-2: Sandpaper abrasives are finer than file teeth.

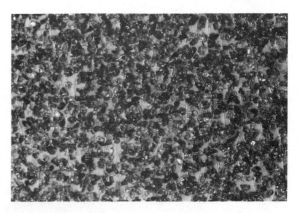

Figure 20-3: Each piece of grit on a piece of sandpaper is like a tiny tooth. Its grit is determined by the number of grains that will fit evenly on a square inch.

Figure 20-4: Grit size is printed on the back of the sandpaper. Sometimes the difference in grit is too fine to see with the naked eye. (3-M Company)

abrasive is called its grit and is measured by how many grains will fit on a square inch. Grits range from very coarse to very fine (figure 20-3). The grit size is printed on the back of the sandpaper (figure 20-4).

Grit sizes are marked in regular numbers (mesh sizes) such as 50, 150, and 220. Another method is to use aught (zero) sizes. Thus 50 grit is 1/0 (one aught), 150 grit is 4/0 (four aught), and 220 grit is 6/0 (six aught).

The higher the grit number, the finer the sandpaper. Lower numbers are coarser sandpaper.

	MESH NUMBER SIZES	AUGHT SIZES
	220	6/0
FINE	180	5/0
	150	4/0
	120	3/0
MEDIUM	100	2/0
	80	0
	60	1/2
COARSE	50	1
	40	1-1/2

SELF CHECK

1. What are the two kinds of abrasive material used in sandpaper?
2. What is the difference between garnet and aluminum oxide?
3. Which abrasive is most commonly used by woodworkers?
4. Which is coarser: 150 grit or 60 grit?

Hand sanding takes hard work and patience. The result of good sanding is a slick surface that is the first thing to be felt and seen in any piece of good woodwork. And a poor sanding job stands out like a sore thumb.

Hand sanding (figure 21-1) is made easier by remembering to:

● Select the right grit for the job
● Go to finer grits in steps (do not jump from coarse to fine without using medium)
● Always sand with the grain
● Hand sand only to smooth a cut surface. (Do not attempt to hand sand a piece of wood down to the right size.)

Figure 21-2: For most sanding jobs, large sheets of sandpaper can be torn into smaller sheets.

Figure 21-1: Hand sanding is usually done by wrapping the sandpaper around a block of wood. Always sand with the grain.

Figure 21-3: Sandpaper is made more flexible by "breaking the backing," which means pulling the back of the sandpaper over the edge of a block of wood.

Selecting the right grit means to use a coarse grit such as 60, to remove tool marks. This grit levels out surfaces cut by handsaws and band saws. For sanding surfaces that were pre-machined use 80 or 100 grit. Before moving on to medium grit papers, be sure all saw or machine marks are removed.

Going to finer grits in steps is the process of sanding the sanding marks. Each grit leaves scratches in the work. Going from 50 to 100 grit will leave finer marks, but it skips many grits. Coarser grits cut faster. So going from 50 to 60 to 80 to 100 grit is faster than going directly from 50 to 100. Finer grits clog faster, too. Heavy sanding of coarse work with fine sandpaper will clog the fine paper.

All sanding should be done with the grain, rubbing the sandpaper back and forth in the same direction as the grain. This leaves fewer obvious scratches on the wood. Good sanding is done firmly and evenly.

Sandpaper comes in 9 x 11 inch sheets. These may be torn into four equal parts (figure 21-2) for more economical use. Each piece can be made more flexible by pulling it (grit side up) across a board edge (figure 21-3).

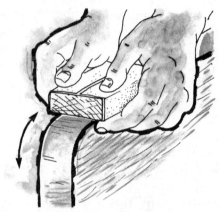

Figure 21-5: A sanding block can be used to sand an outside curve.

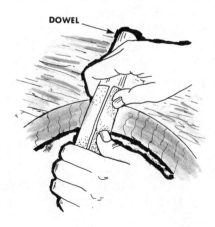

Figure 21-6: An inside curve can be sanded with a piece of sandpaper wrapped around a dowel.

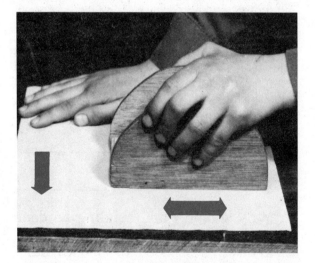

Figure 21-4: Flat surfaces are sanded with a sanding block. When the piece to be sanded is very small, the sandpaper is held to the bench and the piece is moved on the sandpaper.

When sanding flat surfaces, use a sanding block. You can make your own sanding block by cutting a piece of wood to an easy-to-hold size. The sandpaper is held tightly to the block with thumb and fingers. The block is pressed firmly against the workpiece while it is rubbed back and forth with the grain. Never tack the sandpaper to the sanding block. Never sand across the grain. Sanding across the grain tears the wood fibers. Torn wood fibers will be visible when the wood is stained or finished.

Small flat surfaces and square edges are difficult to sand. Sanding usually rounds off the corners. To prevent damaging corners or edges, rub the work against the sandpaper. This is done by laying a full sheet of sandpaper on the workbench and moving the piece to be sanded against it (figure 21-4).

Sanding an outside curve can be done with a sanding block (figure 21-5). To sand an inside or irregular curve, a round dowel may be used for the sanding block (figure 21-6).

Small dents in wood can be raised with a few drops of water. This will swell the wood fibers. After the area dries it can be lightly sanded (figure 21-7). Filler may be used in deep dents. But usually filler will be visible after staining or finishing.

A good sanding job is finished by rounding the edges and corners of the work with fine sandpaper (figure 21-8). About a 1/16 inch radius is all that is necessary.

The final step is to inspect the surfaces carefully in good light. Be sure

Figure 21-7: After the dents in the wood have been repaired, it can be lightly sanded with fine sandpaper.

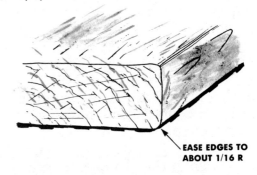

EASE EDGES TO
ABOUT 1/16 R

Figure 21-8: A good sanding job includes rounding the edges and corners of the work to about a 1/16 inch radius.

that all marks are removed. End grains should be slick and only the natural color and markings in the wood itself should be visible. Hand sanding is a tough job, but well worth the effort.

SELF CHECK

1. Why should hand sanding be done with the grain?
2. What grit is used to smooth hand sawn surfaces?
3. How can small dents be raised on wood surfaces?
4. How is an inside curve sanded?

Portable electric sanders are used to sand large, flat areas. They are seldom used to sand edges or small end grain surfaces. The two most common types of portable electric sanders are:

● Pad sanders
● Belt sanders

<u>Pad sanders</u> (figure 22-1) may have a circular (orbital) or a back and forth sanding action. The size of the sanding surface, speeds, and length of stroke (back and forth movement) vary from sander to sander. These are easy tools to use (figure 22-2). Safety rules (figure 22-3) are simple to follow.

<u>Belt sanders</u> (figure 22-4) are heavy and fast cutting. An endless cloth belt

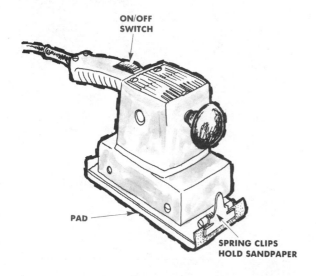

Figure 22-1: Pad sanders may have a circular or back and forth sanding action.

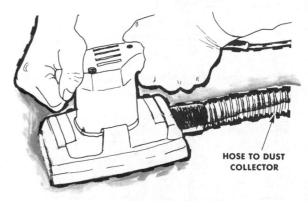

Figure 22-2: Some sanders have their own system for collecting sawdust.

●WEAR EYE PROTECTION.

●WEAR A DUST MASK (RESPIRATOR) IF NECESSARY.

●CLAMP YOUR WORK.

●LIFT THE SANDER OFF THE WORK BENCH BEFORE STARTING OR STOPPING.

●HOLD THE TOOL WITH BOTH HANDS.

●APPLY LITTLE DOWNWARD PRESSURE.

Figure 22-3: Safety rules for pad sanders are simple to follow.

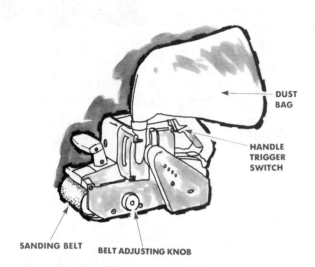

Figure 22-4: Belt sanders are heavy and fast cutting.

Figure 22-5: Be careful when you use a belt sander. Careless use will ruin the wood you are sanding.

is driven by two wheels. The outside of the belt is coated with abrasive and this does the sanding. Belts come in different lengths and widths. Some belt sanders even have their own vacuum system for collecting sanding dust.

Because belt sanders cut wood so fast, careless use can cause mistakes that will instantly ruin a project.

To use a belt sander, it is turned on and held until the belt is running at full speed. It is then used like a sanding block. The sander is stroked back and forth on the work with the grain of the wood (figure 22-5). If held in one place, it will dig a hole. Tipping the sander

to the side will cause a gouge. The sander is lifted off the work before it is turned off.

SELF CHECK

1. What are the two common types of portable power sanders?
2. Which sander is easiest to use?
3. What happens when a belt sander is held in one place?
4. How does the operator avoid breathing sanding dust?

Heavy sanding machines are used in most shops. They are like portable electric sanders but are stronger and are bolted to a workbench or mounted on their own stands. The three most common sanding machines are:

- Belt sanders
- Disk sanders
- Drum sanders

Belt sanding machines (figure 23-1) are like portable belt sanders. Mounted vertically on the bench, the belt sanding machine is larger and easier to use than the portable belt sander. The main use of belt sanding machines is smoothing saw cuts on the edges of boards. Six inch wide belts are commonly used.

Disk sanders (figure 23-2) have a large, flat disk with sandpaper glued to it. The disk is commonly 12 inches in diameter. Sanding must be done against the half of the disk that rotates toward the ground.

Drum sanders (figure 23-3) are usually drill press attachments. They are used to sand inside curves on board edges (figure 23-4). Different drum sizes are used since the drum must be smaller than the curve to be sanded. The work is fed against the rotation of the sanding drum.

When sanding with belt and disk sanders, hold the work flat on the table (figure 23-5). Sanding small work should be avoided because the operator's hands and fingers will be too close to the sanding disk or belt. Both disk and belt sanding machines are used on outside curves (figure 23-6).

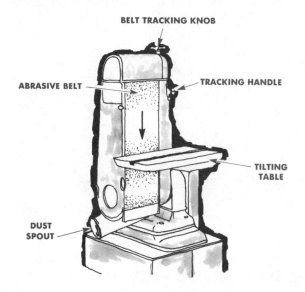

Figure 23-1: Belt sanding machines are like portable belt sanders mounted vertically on the bench.

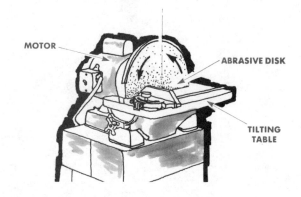

Figure 23-2: Disk sanding is done against the half of the disk that rotates toward the floor.

Figure 23-3: Drum sanders are usually drill press attachments.

Figure 23-4: Drum sanders are used to sand inside curves. They come in different sizes. A drum sander must be smaller than the curve being sanded.

Figure 23-5: By holding the work flat on the table when sanding with belt and disk sanders, the operator avoids rounding the edges.

Figure 23-6: Both disk and belt sanding machines are used on outside curves.

Different grits are used on sanding machines. Coarse grits remove a lot of wood quickly. Finer grits are used to prepare the work for hand finishing. Most sanding machines leave cross grain scratches.

Figure 23-7: Sanding machines are used to round corners.

Figure 23-8: Small miters can be shaped with disk or belt sanders.

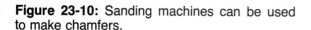

Figure 23-10: Sanding machines can be used to make chamfers.

Figure 23-9: Bevels like this can be done on sanding machines.

Sanding machines are used to round corners (figure 23-7), make small miters (figure 23-8), and bevels (figure 23-9), and make chamfers (figure 23-10).

SELF CHECK

1. List three kinds of sanding machines.
2. Why is sanding small work dangerous?
3. What are safety glasses used for?
4. Which machine is used to sand inside curves?

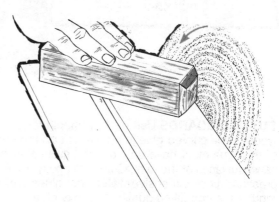

FASTENING

4

The pieces of all woodworking projects that involve more than one part must be fastened together. Choosing the right joint, using the right fastener, and clamping glued joints correctly are skills that all woodworkers need.

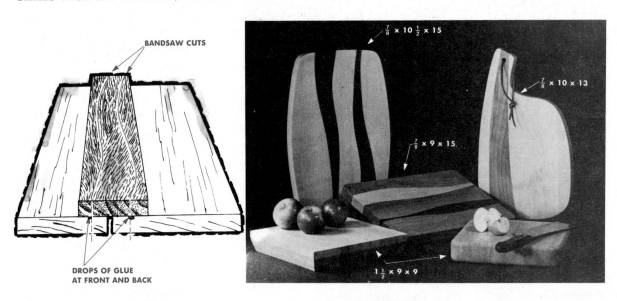

BANDSAW CUTS

DROPS OF GLUE
AT FRONT AND BACK

$\frac{7}{8}$ x 10 $\frac{1}{2}$ x 15

$\frac{7}{8}$ x 10 x 13

$\frac{7}{8}$ x 9 x 15

1 $\frac{1}{2}$ x 9 x 9

CUTTING BOARDS Use birch or maple for the light colored woods. Cherry and walnut are the darker woods. The curved glue joints are cut on the band saw by stack cutting as shown in the sketch. Joints of this type must have only gradual curves, without sharp changes in direction. Do not sand the band sawn surfaces of the joint. Glue with epoxy adhesives. Coat each surface generously and use moderate pressure. Less expensive waterproof glues can be used for straight edge-to-edge joints. These do not require the gap filling quality of epoxy glue.

The place where two or more pieces of wood are fit together is called a joint. Sometimes the way the wood fits together will hold the joint together. More often joints are fastened with glue, nails, or screws. The most common woodworking joints are:

- Butt joints
- Miter joints
- Rabbet joints
- Dado joints
- Tongue and groove joints
- Lap joints
- Mortise and tenon joints

Butt joints (figure 24-1) are simply two pieces of wood "butted" together. Butt joints are the easiest—and the weakest—of all joints. When it is pos-sible, the grain of both pieces of wood should run in the same direction. Glued joints are strongest when the grains of the wood in all pieces face in the same direction.

All joints are strongest when two flat, square surfaces fit tightly against each other. Hand sanding rounds corners and edges. It should be avoided at joints. End grain butts are the weakest of all the joints.

Miter joints (figure 24-2) are like butt joints. The angle of the wood is usually cut with a saw and miter box (figure 24-3).

Rabbet joints (figure 24-4) are used to make right angles and join wood pieces of different thickness. Similar to

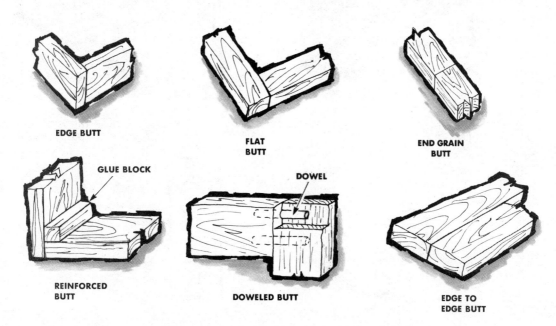

EDGE BUTT

FLAT
BUTT

END GRAIN
BUTT

GLUE BLOCK

REINFORCED
BUTT

DOWEL

DOWELED BUTT

EDGE TO
EDGE BUTT

Figure 24-1: Two pieces of wood "butted" together make a butt joint.

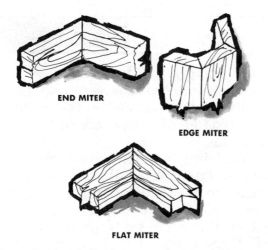

END MITER

EDGE MITER

FLAT MITER

Figure 24-2: Miter joints are similar to butt joints. They are joined at an angle.

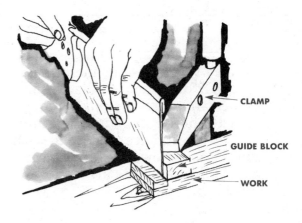

CLAMP

GUIDE BLOCK

WORK

Figure 24-5: Rabbet joints may be cut with a router, chisel, or saw.

Figure 24-3: A saw and miter box are necessary to cut perfect angles for the miter joint.

DADO JOINT

Figure 24-6: A dado joint is made by cutting a slot. Then a second board is fit into the slot.

NAILS

RABBET JOINTS

Figure 24-4: Rabbet joints can be used to join woods of different thicknesses.

the butt joint, rabbet joints are used to make boxes, cabinets, and furniture. They are cut with a router, chisel, or saw (figure 24-5).

Dado joints (figure 24-6) are made by cutting a slot across the grain. The second board fits into the slot. The dado slot may be routed or cut by hand with a saw and cleaned out with a chisel (figure 24-7).

Tongue and groove joints (figure 24-8) are not as strong as edge to edge butt joints. The major use of this type of joint is to align long wood pieces, such as wood flooring.

Lap joints (figure 24-9) include the corner lap joint and the cross lap joint. Both boards are rabbetted to half their thickness. The corner lap joint is stronger than a butt joint, and the cross lap joint is harder to move.

Mortise and tenon joints (figure 24-10) are difficult to make. Both parts must be cut to fit exactly in position. Mortise and tenon joints are used mostly on fine furniture and cabinets.

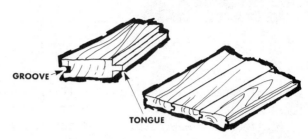

Figure 24-8: Tongue and groove joints are weak but provide a convenient method of aligning long pieces of wood.

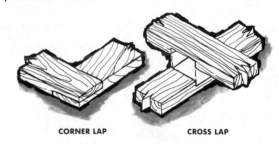

Figure 24-9: The two lap joints are the corner lap joint and the cross lap joint.

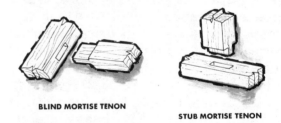

Figure 24-10: Mortise and tenon joints must be cut together perfectly to fit.

Figure 24-7: Dado slots are cut with a router or by hand with a saw. The saw cut must be cleaned out with a chisel.

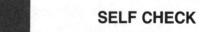

SELF CHECK

1. Which joint is easiest to make?
2. What is a rabbet joint?
3. Which joint is used for wood flooring?
4. What is the advantage of a lap joint?

Glues are also called adhesives. This is because it makes two or more pieces of wood adhere (stick) to each other. There are other ways to fasten wood together, but gluing makes the strongest joints.

There are different kinds of glues with special properties. But the three most common glues in woodworking are:
- White liquid glue
- Powder glue (resin glue)
- Epoxy glue

White liquid glue (figure 25-1), also known as polyvinyl, is the most popular. Good for all indoor wood-to-wood gluing, it is easy and safe to use. White glue is weakened by moisture and high temperatures. When it dries it is rubbery and difficult to sand from wood surfaces.

Powder glues (figure 25-2) come dry. Water is mixed with the glue until it is lump free and like heavy cream. Once mixed, powder glue may not be stored. Powder glue may be either casein or plastic resin (also called urea resin). Only some plastic resin glues are waterproof. But all powder glues resist water better than white liquid glue. Another feature of powder glues is that they dry very hard. Saws and planes may be dulled from cutting hardened powder glue. However, powder glue is easier to sand than white liquid glue.

Figure 25-1: White liquid glue comes in plastic dispensers. It is also called polyvinyl glue.

Figure 25-2: Powder glues must be mixed with water before use.

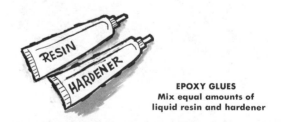

EPOXY GLUES
Mix equal amounts of liquid resin and hardener

Figure 25-3: Epoxy glue usually comes in two tubes and must be mixed.

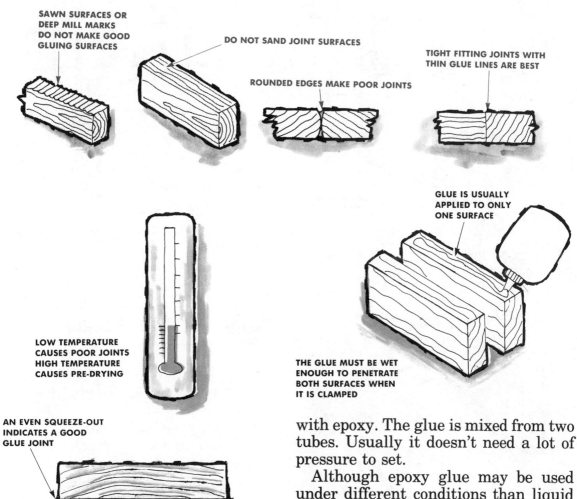

SAWN SURFACES OR DEEP MILL MARKS DO NOT MAKE GOOD GLUING SURFACES

DO NOT SAND JOINT SURFACES

ROUNDED EDGES MAKE POOR JOINTS

TIGHT FITTING JOINTS WITH THIN GLUE LINES ARE BEST

GLUE IS USUALLY APPLIED TO ONLY ONE SURFACE

LOW TEMPERATURE CAUSES POOR JOINTS HIGH TEMPERATURE CAUSES PRE-DRYING

THE GLUE MUST BE WET ENOUGH TO PENETRATE BOTH SURFACES WHEN IT IS CLAMPED

AN EVEN SQUEEZE-OUT INDICATES A GOOD GLUE JOINT

PRESSURE MUST BE MAINTAINED UNTIL THE GLUE HAS SET

Figure 25-4: The general rules for gluing are the same for all glues.

Epoxy glues (figure 25-3) are also known as two-part glues. Epoxies glue metal, plastics, and woods and are waterproof. Gaps between the two surfaces being glued can also be filled in with epoxy. The glue is mixed from two tubes. Usually it doesn't need a lot of pressure to set.

Although epoxy glue may be used under different conditions than liquid or powder glue, the general rules for good gluing are the same for all glues (figure 25-4).

Aside from the glue, the most important part of good gluing is clamping the work solidly. The basic clamps and their uses are:
● Bar clamps for edge-to-edge gluing and assembly work (figure 25-5)
● Hand screw clamps for face-to-face gluing (figure 25-6)
● C-clamps for gluing face-to-face (figure 25-7)

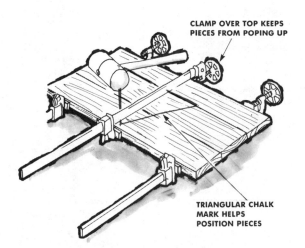

Figure 25-5: Edge-to-edge gluing is done with bar-clamps.

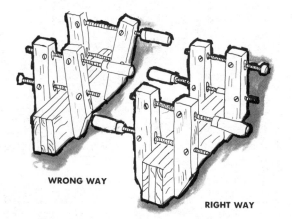

Figure 25-6: Screw-clamps hold boards face-to-face.

Figure 25-7: C-clamps are also used to hold pieces face-to-face for gluing. Wood scraps protect against denting the work.

SELF CHECK

1. List three types of glue.
2. What will weaken white liquid glue?
3. What glue dulls tools?
4. What are two reasons for using epoxy glue?

Nails (figure 26-1) are made from wire. Nail sizes are indicated by the term "penny". Examples are two-penny, four-penny, and so on. The word "penny" is written as a "d" (2d, 4d). The larger the penny number, the bigger the nail. Figure 26-2 gives lengths for different size (penny) nails.

There are many types of nails available for use. Special nails are made for special jobs. Selecting the kind of nail to use depends upon:

● The size of material (thin or thick)
● The kind of material (hard or soft)
● The kind of work being done (finished or rough)

The most basic kinds of nails are:

Common Nails—used in carpentry and construction to nail heavy planks and frame members.

Box Nails—like common nails but have thinner heads and diameters. Box nails are used where appearance is not important.

Finishing Nails—used where appearance is important. The small head is usually driven below the wood surface.

Figure 26-1: Nails are made from wire.

PENNY Size															
2d	3d	4d	5d	6d	7d	8d	9d	10d	12d	16d	20d	30d	40d	50d	60d
1"	$1\frac{1}{4}$	$1\frac{1}{2}$	$1\frac{3}{4}$	2	$2\frac{1}{4}$	$2\frac{1}{2}$	$2\frac{3}{4}$	3	$3\frac{1}{4}$	$3\frac{1}{2}$	4	$4\frac{1}{2}$	5	$5\frac{1}{2}$	6
ACTUAL Length															

Figure 26-2: This nail chart shows the length of each penny size nail.

Figure 26-3: Starting a nail is done by holding it steady and lightly pounding it in till it will stand by itself.

Figure 26-4: The hammer handles easiest by grasping it by the end.

Brads—small, thin finishing nails that are sized in length by inches. They range from one-quarter to two inches in length. Brads are used for nailing thin materials.

Hammers are used to drive and pull nails of every kind except "finger nails". Claw hammer sizes are determined by the weight of their heads. Thirteen and sixteen ounce are the most popular sizes.

Driving nails is done by steadying the nail with one hand while grasping the hammer handle at the end in your other hand (figure 26-3 and 26-4). The

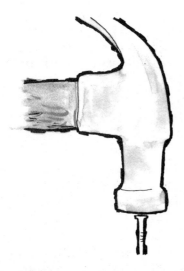

Figure 26-5: The hammer should strike the nail squarely. Not striking the nail head squarely may start the nail at an angle, damage the head, or bend the nail.

Figure 26-7: Nails hold best when they are driven at right angles to the wood grain. They hold because the wood fibers wedge against the nail.

Figure 26-6: Finishing nails are set below the wood surface with a nail set.

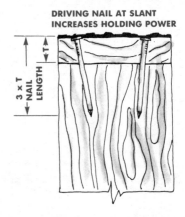

Figure 26-8: Nails should be driven into end grain at a slant.

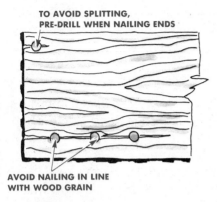

Figure 26-9: Different techniques help prevent splitting the board.

Figure 26-10: The claw is used to pull nails.

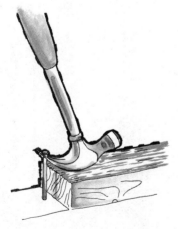

Figure 26-11: A block of wood under a hammer provides leverage and protects the surface of the wood.

nail is tapped lightly to start it. Strike the nail by hitting the head squarely (figure 26-5).

Heads of common and box nails are driven slightly into the surface. Finishing nails and brads are driven almost to the surface. Then they are set below the surface of the wood with a proper size nail set (figure 26-6).

Nails hold best when driven at right angles to the wood grain fibers (figure 26-7). Nails driven into the end grain (parallel to the fibers) do not hold as well. Nails hold better in end grain when driven at a slant (figure 26-8).

Hardwoods and thin stock may be nailed by pre-drilling small holes. This helps the nails go in easier and prevents splitting. Avoid driving nails close together in line with the grain. This may also cause splitting (figure 26-9).

The correct way to pull nails is shown in figure 26-10. Use a block under the hammer to gain leverage and protect work surfaces (figure 26-11).

SELF CHECK

1. What is the length of a six-penny nail?
2. Do box nails have thinner heads than common nails?
3. What are two types of nails used for finish work?
4. How is the size of a hammer determined?

Wood screws (figure 27-1) are described by:
- Length in inches
- Diameter—gage number
- Type of head—flat, round, oval or pan
- Kind of material—steel, plated, brass

Screws are available in most <u>lengths</u> in steps of one-eighth inch up to one inch and in steps of one quarter inch up to three inches. <u>Diameters</u> are given in gage numbers from zero to thirty. The larger the number, the larger the diameter of the shank. Screws also have heads with either straight slots

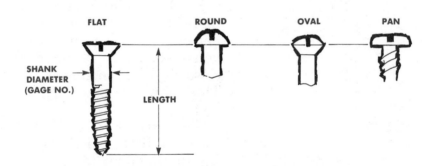

Figure 27-1: Wood screws are described by length, head type, diameter, and material they are made of.

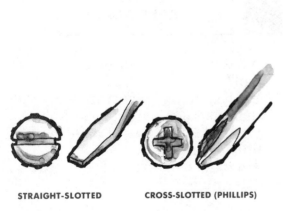

Figure 27-2: The type of slot in the screw head may be either straight-slot or cross-slot.

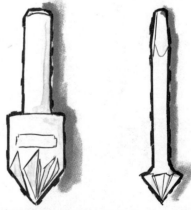

Figure 27-3: Countersink bits make it possible to bury flat head and oval head screws flush in the wood.

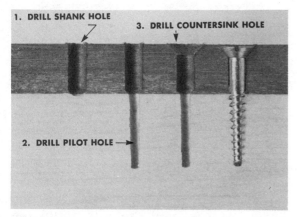

Figure 27-4: The steps in drilling and counter-sinking a screw hole.

or cross slots (called Phillip's heads), figure 27-2.

Flat head and oval head screws are tapered under the head to fit into a countersunk hole. Flat head screws are used where the head must be flush with the surface or below it. With oval head screws, only the beveled part of the head is countersunk. Special bits and drills (figure 27-3) are used to make countersunk holes.

Round head and pan head screws are used where greater holding power is needed. The heads are usually left visible above the surface.

Most screws are made of steel and brass. Some have plated finishes. Nickel, blued, chrome, and galvanized are some examples.

Screws to be driven into the edge grain should be twice as long as the thickness of the wood piece to be fastened. Screws driven into end grain should be three times as long.

Drilling the right size <u>screw holes</u> (figure 27-4) begins with the shank

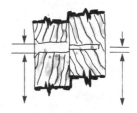

NO. OF SCREW		SHANK CLEARANCE HOLE	PILOT HOLE	
			SOFTWOOD	HARDWOOD
0	•	1/16	1/64	1/32
1	•	5/64	1/32	1/32
2	•	3/32	1/32	3/64
3	•	7/64	3/64	1/16
4	•	7/64	3/64	1/16
5	•	1/8	1/16	5/64
6	•	9/64	1/16	5/64
7	•	5/32	1/16	3/32
8	•	11/64	5/64	3/32
9	•	3/16	5/64	7/64
10	•	3/16	3/32	7/64
11	•	13/64	3/32	1/8
12	•	7/32	7/64	1/8
14	•	1/4	7/64	9/64

Figure 27-5: Hole sizes for softwoods and hardwoods may vary a little.

hole. Use a drill size large enough to let the shank slip into the hole (figure 27-5). Drill a pilot hole if one is needed. Soft woods like pine do not require pilot holes. Medium woods like mahogany, butternut and willow should have small pilot holes. Pilot holes help guide the screw.

STANDARD SLOTTED
SCREW DRIVER

CROSS-SLOT
SCREW DRIVER
(PHILLIPS)

SCREW DRIVER
FOR HAND BRACE

Figure 27-6: The proper screwdriver makes setting the screw easier.

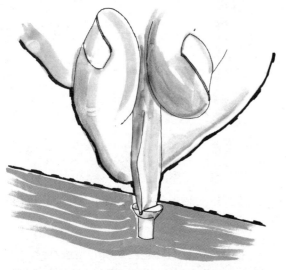

Figure 27-7: The tip should fit the slot snugly.

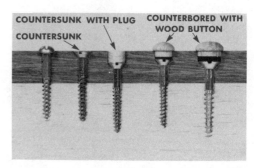

COUNTERSUNK WITH PLUG   COUNTERBORED WITH WOOD BUTTON

COUNTERSUNK

Figure 27-8: A few of the ways to set and cover screws.

Setting screws is done with a screw driver (figure 27-6) that fits snugly in the slot (figure 27-7). Turn the screw until the two pieces are drawn tightly together. Further turning will strip the threads in the pilot hole and the screw will not hold. Some of the ways to set and cover screws are shown in figure 27-8.

SELF CHECK

1. List the four screw specifications.
2. How long should screws be when they are installed in end grain?
3. What tool is used to set flat head screws flush to the surface?
4. What is counterboring?

FINISHING

Finishing is the final woodworking step. Finishes protect and enhance the natural qualities of the wood. They should be chosen carefully, and the manufacturer's directions should be followed closely.

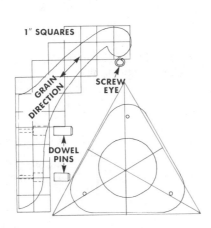

1" SQUARES

GRAIN DIRECTION

SCREW EYE

DOWEL PINS

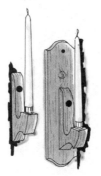

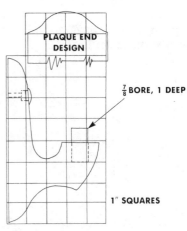

PLAQUE END DESIGN

$\frac{7}{8}$ BORE, 1 DEEP

1" SQUARES

CANDLE SCONCE in stained pine can be made with or without a three-quarter by four by fifteen inch plaque. Use one-half inch diameter screw hole buttons to hide counterbored screws. Brass candle cups shown are optional.

WOOD FINISHING

Figure 28-1: Although expensive, when used properly, aerosol spray finishes give good finishing results.

Figure 28-2: Always store used rags in an approved metal container.

PINCH BRISTLES

Figure 28-3: Careful pinching out of excess solvent from the brush guarantees the brush can be used again.

Finishes protect and improve the natural beauty of wood. But so many kinds of finishes are available that even professional woodworkers have a hard time making a choice.

When choosing an indoor finish, it should have these advantages:

- Easy to apply
- Works fast
- No special equipment necessary for application
- Professionals and beginners should get similar results

Figure 28-4: Cleaning the brush with soap and water is important.

Figure 28-5: Before putting a brush away, wrap the bristles in absorbent paper.

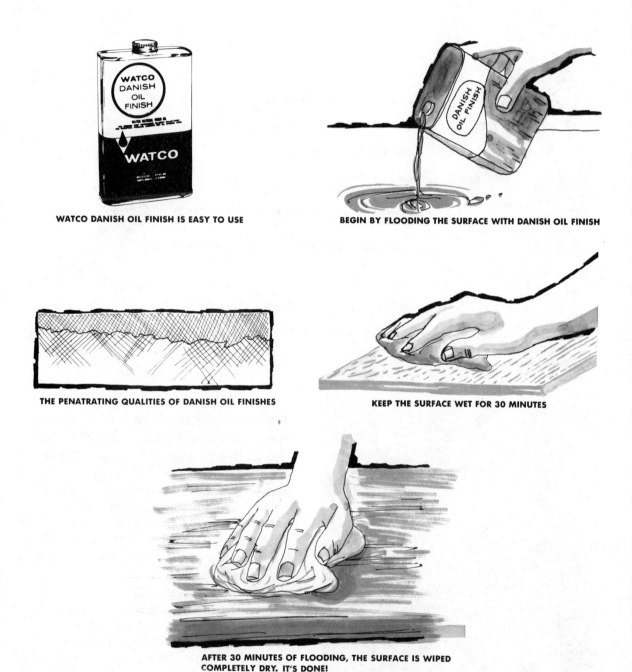

WATCO DANISH OIL FINISH IS EASY TO USE

BEGIN BY FLOODING THE SURFACE WITH DANISH OIL FINISH

THE PENATRATING QUALITIES OF DANISH OIL FINISHES

KEEP THE SURFACE WET FOR 30 MINUTES

AFTER 30 MINUTES OF FLOODING, THE SURFACE IS WIPED
COMPLETELY DRY. IT'S DONE!

Figure 28-6: The steps for applying Watco Danish Oil Finish and 5 Minute Wood Stain. Always read, and follow, the manufacturer's directions.

1 SAND RAW WOOD WITH 220 GRIT GARNET PAPER.

2 APPLY SEALACELL (NO. 1 CAN) WITH CLOTH. COAT GENEROUSLY, LET DRY OVER-NIGHT.

3 BUFF LIGHTLY WITH FINE STEEL WOOD. WIPE CLEAN WITH CLOTH.

4 APPLY THIN COAT OF VARNOWAX (NO. 2 CAN) IN A CIRCULAR MOTION. WIPE OUT WITH THE GRAIN. DO NOT SATURATE CLOTH. ALLOW TWELVE HOURS TO DRY.

5 BUFF LIGHTLY WITH STEEL WOOL. APPLY ROYAL FINISH (NO. 3 CAN) IN THE SAME MANNER AS VARNOWAX.

6 APPLY ADDITIONAL COATS OF ROYAL FINISH TO INCREASE DEPTH AND GLOSS AS DESIRED.

Figure 28-7: The steps for applying Sealacell, a penetrating natural finish. Always read, and follow, the manufacturer's directions.

Figure 28-8: Water based stains made of vinyl and latex are applied with a damp rag.

Fine finishing cannot be achieved even with a super miracle finish unless the surfaces are <u>perfectly sanded.</u> All machine marks, dents, cross grain scratches, and glue spots must be removed. All nail holes must be filled. Wood surfaces must be fine sanded with at least 150 grit sandpaper. Then, the finish must be tested on a scrap of the same kind of wood.

<u>Special precautions</u> must be taken when finishing bowls or wood that come into contact with food. The safest finishes are vegetable cooking oils such as corn oil, olive oil, or peanut oil. Peanut oil is best because it never turns rancid. Rub as much oil into the wood as it will take. Then wipe it dry.

Figure 28-9: When you brush on a stain, work from the center to the edges and overlap your strokes.

Aerosol spray finishes (figure 28-1) are the most expensive method of finishing wood. Each spray can has instructions for use and safety precautions to be taken.

Finishes used outdoors are decayed by moisture and baked by the sun's rays. All woods used in birdhouses or planters will turn a silvery gray, and some kinds will rot away if nothing is put on them. Clear natural finishes like varnish do not last long. Paint, enamel, and stain last longer.

Cleaning brushes is necessary. The steps for cleaning a brush are:
● Remove excess finish from the brush with rags or with scrap paper
● Rinse in solvent (different ones for different finishes)
● Pinch out all the excess solvent (figure 28-3)
● Clean brush with warm water and a bar of soap (figure 28-4)
● Shape the bristles
● Wrap the brush in absorbent paper toweling and hold in place with a rubberband (figure 28-5)

For best results, follow the manufacturer's directions. Typical directions are shown in figures 28-6 and 28-7.

Stains enhance the natural beauty of wood grain. They are applied to the raw wood with a rag (figure 28-8) or a brush (figure 28-9).

SELF CHECK

1. What are two reasons for finishing wood?
2. What is a good finish for salad bowls and cutting boards?
3. Do outdoor projects need a finish?
4. Clear, natural finishes are not good on outdoor projects. Why?

Besides nails and screws, other kinds of hardware are useful in shop projects. The most common pieces are:

● Screw eyes and hooks
● Hangers
● Candle cups
● Sheet acrylic plastic
● Protective felt
● Lamp parts

Screw eyes and hooks (figure 29-1) are good for hanging signs and bird houses. Cup hooks hold cups and other things. Shoulder hooks are good for making racks.

Hangers (figures 29-2 and 29-3) help to hang shelves, plaques, and picture frames.

Candle cups (figure 29-4) hold standard candles. They are available in metal or unfinished wood.

Sheet acrylic plastic (figure 29-5) may be bought at most hardware stores. This material is very good for

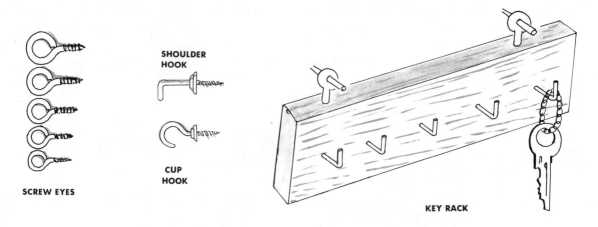

Figure 29-1: Screw eyes and hooks hold things suspended.

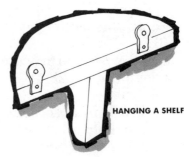

Figure 29-2: Hangers are used on a number of objects.

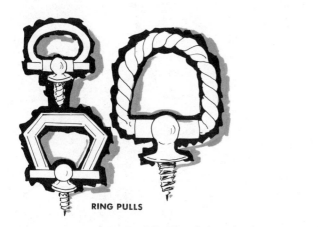

RING PULLS

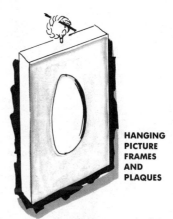

HANGING
PICTURE
FRAMES
AND
PLAQUES

Figure 29-3: Like most attaching hardware, hangers come in sizes that match the need of the individual job.

METAL

WOOD

Figure 29-4: Candle cups hold standard size candles.

ACRYLIC PLASTIC SHEET

PICTURE FRAME "GLASS"

ROLLS

DISKS AND PADS

BOTTOM OF
TABLE LAMP

Figure 29-5: Sheet acrylic plastic may be cut with a fine-toothed saw.

Figure 29-6: Felt is used on the bottoms of projects to protect table tops.

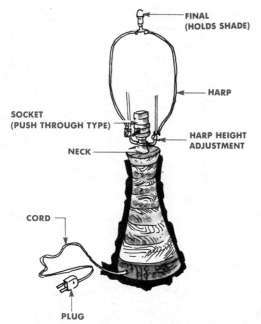

Figure 29-7: Lamps are always popular projects because they are useful. The harp holds the lamp shade. But many shades today are made to clamp onto the light bulb.

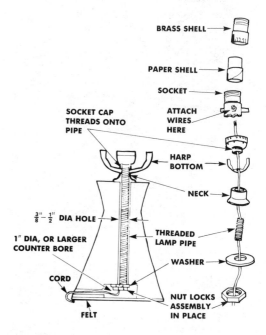

Figure 29-8: Interior lamp assembly.

the glass part of oval and round picture frames. Cut it with a fine tooth saw.

Protective felt (figure 29-6) comes in rolls, disks or pads. Use it to protect tables from the bottoms of projects. Die cut pieces have self-gluing backs.

Lamp parts (figures 29-7 and 29-8) are used in making several kinds of projects.

SELF CHECK

1. List two kinds of picture frame or plaque hangers.
2. Which hanger is used to hang a small shelf?
3. What is felt used for?
4. How can acrylic plastic be cut?

Advanced machines make woodworking easier and more fun. However, they are hazardous to use, and should only be used with your instructor's approval.

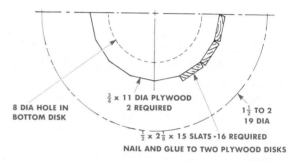

8 DIA HOLE IN BOTTOM DISK

$\frac{3}{4}$ x 11 DIA PLYWOOD 2 REQUIRED

$1\frac{1}{2}$ TO 2 19 DIA

$\frac{1}{2}$ x $2\frac{1}{8}$ x 15 SLATS - 16 REQUIRED

NAIL AND GLUE TO TWO PLYWOOD DISKS

ROUND TABLE with a sixteen piece slat base is shown in butternut. This project is easier to make than it looks. Carefully stack cut two, sixteen sided disks of three-quarter inch plywood. Tip: rip the slats about one-sixteenth inch wider. Hand plane each to fit as you assemble with glue and finish nails.

TURNED WEED POTS range from two to five inches in diameter and two to eight inches high. All are spindle turned on the lathe. Holes are drilled with the drill press. (Turnings by Bob Spielman)

TURNED CANDLE HOLDERS in teak are five and seven inches tall. Base and top diameters are three inches.

The table saw (figure 30-1) has a circular blade. The blade diameter determines the size of the machine. Most schools have ten or twelve inch saws. Figure 30-1 shows the basic parts and adjustments. You will use the table saw for ripping and crosscutting. The three basic kinds of circular blades are shown in figure 30-2.

Be sure to observe the precautions given in figure 30-3 when you use the table saw.

Ripping is sawing with the grain to make a board a certain width. The stock is always guided against the rip fence.

Raise or lower the blade so it is no more than one-quarter inch above the thickness of your board (figure 30-4). You do not need to draw a layout line on your board. Adjust the fence for the width of cut as shown in figure 30-5. Lock the fence. Put the guard in position (and your goggles on too). Stand close to the machine and to one side of the blade. This will put you out of the "firing line" should a piece be thrown back (kick back) from the saw.

Start the machine. Feed the work against the fence and into the blade (figure 30-6). Complete the cut, pushing the board past the blade (figure 30-7). Push it off the table to be taken by a helper or let it fall onto the floor. Do not pull it back toward you! Shut off the power.

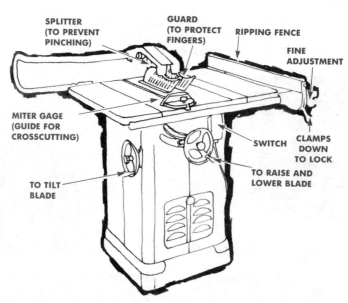

Figure 30-1: The basic parts and adjustments on the table saw make it a key tool for the woodworker.

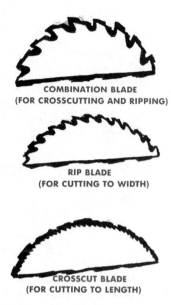

COMBINATION BLADE
(FOR CROSSCUTTING AND RIPPING)

RIP BLADE
(FOR CUTTING TO WIDTH)

CROSSCUT BLADE
(FOR CUTTING TO LENGTH)

Figure 30-2: Different saw blades are used for different cutting jobs.

Ripping narrow pieces four inches or less in width requires special care. You must use a push stick as shown in figure 30-8. Use it to feed the stock past the blade. Hold the push stick at the end of its handle—not low near the blade. Always keep your hands a safe distance (at least six inches) from the blade. If the work does not allow this, do not cut it.

Crosscutting is sawing a piece of wood to length. The fence is not used. Move the fence out of the way or remove it from the machine. The miter gage is used to guide the stock for crosscutting. Mark a cutting line across the width and down the edge of your board.

● DRESS RIGHT, WEAR EYE PROTECTION, TUCK IN LOOSE CLOTHING AND HAIR.

● USE THE GUARD, SPLITTER, AND ANTI-KICKBACK DEVICE.

● DO NOT EXPOSE THE BLADE MORE THAN ONE-QUARTER INCH ABOVE YOUR STOCK THICKNESS.

● USE ONLY THE RIGHT KIND OF BLADE AND BE SURE IT IS SHARP.

● NEVER ATTEMPT TO DO FREE HAND SAWING. ALWAYS USE A GUIDE.

● USE THE RIP FENCE GUIDE FOR RIPPING ONLY.

● ONLY USE THE MITER GAGE GUIDE FOR CROSSCUTTING.

● DO NOT SAW WARPED OR TWISTED BOARDS.

● USE A PUSH STICK FOR RIPPING NARROW BOARDS.

● ALWAYS ALLOW BLADE TO STOP BEFORE REMOVING SCRAPS.

Figure 30-3: The table saw can be a dangerous tool if proper precautions are not taken.

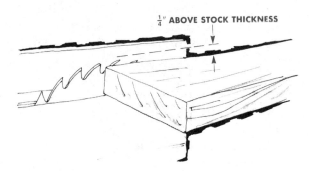

Figure 30-4: With the power off, the blade is raised and lowered so that it cuts only one-quarter of an inch above the stock.

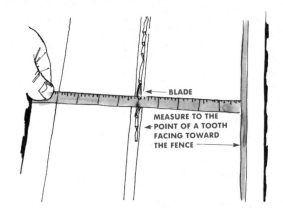

Figure 30-5: The fence controls the width of the cut being made.

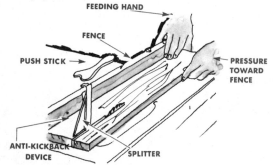

Figure 30-6: Feed the work against the fence and into the blade. (Guard removed to show work more clearly—never operate a table saw without a guard.)

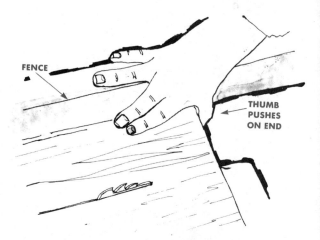

Figure 30-7: Cut wood is always pushed past the blade. It is never pulled back toward the operator. (Guard removed to show work more clearly—never operate a table saw without using a guard.)

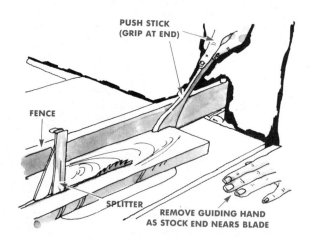

Figure 30-8: A push stick keeps fingers and hands away from the blade on any job. (Guard removed to show work more clearly—never operate a table saw without a guard.)

Before turning the power on, position your board against the miter gage so the layout mark is in line with the blade. Remember to align it so the cut

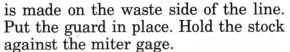

Figure 30-9: Hands and fingers should be kept six inches away from the blade when feeding work into the machine. (Guard removed to show work more clearly—never operate a table saw without a guard.)

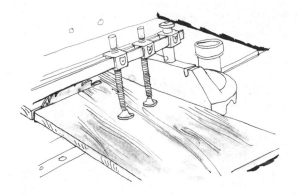

Figure 30-10: A miter gage clamp makes precise cutting easier for beginning students. (Guard removed to show work more clearly—never operate a table saw without a guard.)

is made on the waste side of the line. Put the guard in place. Hold the stock against the miter gage.

Turn on the power. Advance your work into the saw as shown in figure 30-9. At the completion of the cut, slide the stock slightly to the left. Return to the starting position with your wood held tightly against the miter gage. Turn the power off. Wait for the saw blade to stop revolving before you remove the scrap piece. If one is available, you should use a miter gage clamp like shown in figure 30-10.

SELF CHECK

1. What determines the size of a table saw?
2. Name the basic table sawing jobs.
3. How high should the blade height be set above the stock thickness?
4. What must be used to rip narrow boards safely?

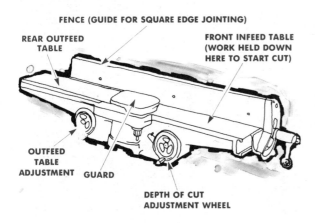

Figure 31-1: The jointer is used for surface work on wood.

The jointer (figure 31-1) is used for surface work. The size of the jointer is determined by the knife lengths in the cutterhead. Six and eight inch sizes are common. Most jointers can make cuts up to 1/16 inch deep (figure 31-2). Use of the jointer requires special safety rules (figure 31-3).

The jointer does two kinds of work:
● Edge jointing
● Face jointing

Edge jointing (figure 31-4) is the process of planing the sawn edge of S2S (surfaced two sides) boards. The jointer

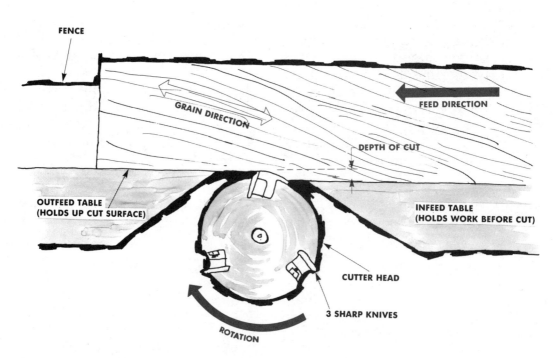

Figure 31-2: Cuts with a jointer are shallow, 1/16 inch deep or less.

- DRESS RIGHT, WEAR EYE PROTECTION, NO LOOSE SLEEVES, SWEATERS, OR JEWELRY.

- STOCK MUST BE TWELVE INCHES OR LONGER.

- HAVE INSTRUCTOR INSPECT YOUR STOCK AND THE JOINTER ADJUSTMENT.

- FEED "WITH THE GRAIN" AS SHOWN IN FIGURE 31-2. THE GRAIN LINES SHOULD SLOPE "DOWN HILL" TOWARD THE TRAILING END OF THE BOARD.

- ALWAYS KEEP HANDS WELL AWAY (FOUR INCHES OR MORE) FROM CUTTING KNIVES.

- BE SURE THE SELF ADJUSTING GUARD COVERS THE CUTTERHEAD.

- DO NOT EDGE JOINT PIECES LESS THAN FOUR INCHES IN WIDTH WITHOUT YOUR INSTRUCTOR'S IMMEDIATE SUPERVISION.

- USE A PUSHER WHEN FACE JOINTING (SEE FIGURE 31-7).

Figure 31-3: Special safety rules for operating a jointer.

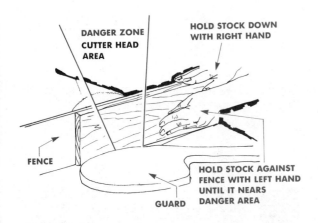

Figure 31-4: For edge jointing, the jointer makes one edge of a board straight and flat for perfect gluing.

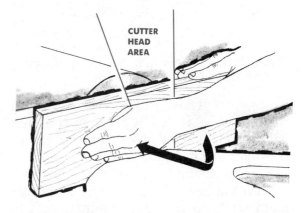

Figure 31-5: Feeding the work through the jointer, the operator moves one hand at a time to keep his fingers clear of the blades.

smoothes, trues, and squares an edge so it is ready for gluing. When two boards have been prepared, they can be glued together edge to edge.

To use the jointer, stand to the left of the infeed table. Press the workpiece against the fence and down. Move your hands one at a time (figure 31-5) to keep your fingers away from the

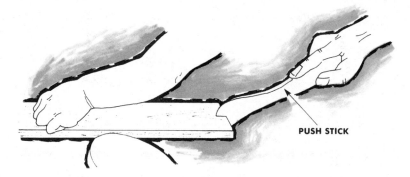

Figure 31-6: A push stick is used to feed narrow stock.

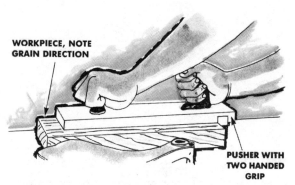

Figure 31-7: A pusher is similar to a push stick, only it is used with both hands.

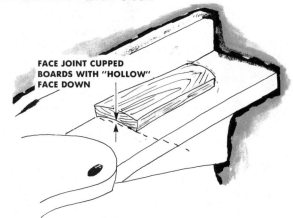

Figure 31-8: Warped or cupped stock is fed through the jointer, face down.

blades. Narrow stock, less than 4 inches wide, is fed with a push stick (figure 31-6). End grain and edges of plywood are not jointed.

Face jointing (figure 31-7) is done with a pusher. The pusher is a special push stick made for face jointing. It is used with two hands. Feeding direction is determined by the grain. The surface to be planed should be flat on the infeed table.

Sometimes rough stock is curved (warped) across its width. This is called "cup". Such stock must be placed on the infeed table with its hollow surface down (figure 31-8).

SELF CHECK

1. What are two kinds of work a jointer is used for?
2. How can you tell the size of a jointer?
3. What is a push stick?
4. What is a pusher?

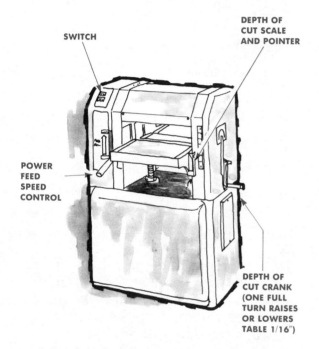

SWITCH

DEPTH OF CUT SCALE AND POINTER

POWER FEED SPEED CONTROL

DEPTH OF CUT CRANK (ONE FULL TURN RAISES OR LOWERS TABLE 1/16")

Figure 32-1: The surface planer is used to make boards smooth and parallel on two sides.

The surface planer (figure 32-1) is used to make rough boards smooth on two sides (S2S). It may also be used to plane boards to equal thicknesses.

The surface planer works by cutting excess wood off the top surface of the board (figure 32-2). Once the wood is started into the machine, it will feed itself.

Planers are described by the size wood they will take. A 13 x 6 inch planer is one which will take that size of wood. Warped wood may be surfaced. But it requires special preparation. Like many woodworking machines, the planer has its own set of safety rules (figure 32-3).

To use the surfacer (figure 32-4) the stock is measured at its thickest end or corner. The table is raised or lowered so the cut will be 1/16 inch or less. The board is lined up so the cut will be with

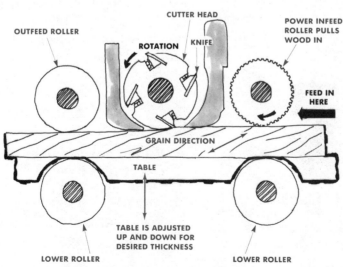

OUTFEED ROLLER

CUTTER HEAD

ROTATION KNIFE

POWER INFEED ROLLER PULLS WOOD IN

FEED IN HERE

GRAIN DIRECTION

TABLE

TABLE IS ADJUSTED UP AND DOWN FOR DESIRED THICKNESS

LOWER ROLLER

LOWER ROLLER

Figure 32-2: The surface planer works like an automatic jointer. Note the direction of the wood grain. It must always face uphill toward the trailing edge.

● DRESS RIGHT! WEAR GOGGLES, TUCK IN LOOSE CLOTHING AND HAIR.

● WOOD MUST BE CLEAN AND SOUND. FREE OF GLUE, SAND, NAILS, FINISHES AND SO ON.

● BOARD MUST BE TWELVE INCHES OR MORE IN LENGTH.

● BOARD MUST HAVE A FLAT SURFACE TO REST FLATLY ON THE TABLE AND LOWER ROLLERS.

● DO NOT FACE CUPPED OR WARPED BOARDS ON THE JOINTER WITHOUT YOUR INSTRUCTOR'S HELP.

● STAND TO THE SIDE WHEN OPERATING.

● DO NOT LOOK INTO THE MACHINE.

● MAKE THIN CUTS, NOT MORE THAN ONE-SIXTEENTH INCH, EACH PASS.

● DO NOT PLANE WOOD TO A FINISHED THICKNESS LESS THAN THREE-EIGHTHS INCH WITHOUT INSTRUCTOR'S APPROVAL.

Figure 32-3: Safety concerns for the surface planer.

Figure 32-4: This operator is using the surface planer correctly. Note the direction in which the wood grain is pointing as well as the operator standing to the side.

Figure 32-5: Wide stock that has been glued edge-to-edge can be planed smooth and parallel on the surface planer. Always remove any excess glue from the stock before you plane it.

the grain. With the power on, the operator stands to one side and feeds the stock flat on the table into the planer. When the rollers grab the stock, it will continue feeding without help.

If the wood is still too thick, it should be fed through again after raising the table 1/16 inch. Edge glued stock usually needs to be planed on both sides (figure 32-5). Plywood, hardboard, or particle board should not be surfaced on the planer. The glue is too hard, and it will dull the planer knives.

SELF CHECK

1. Which surface does the planer cut?
2. Can warped wood be planed?
3. How deep should a surface planer cut?
4. Why isn't plywood run through a surface planer?

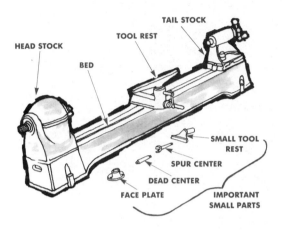

Figure 33-1: The wood lathe has four major parts: the headstock, the bed, the tool rest, and the tailstock.

The wood lathe (figure 33-1) is one of the most interesting woodworking machines to use. Lamps, candle holders, baseball bats, and bowls are made on the lathe. Wood lathes are sized by the maximum diameter that can be turned on them. The 12 inch lathe is a common size. Lathes do two types of work:

● Spindle turning
● Face plate turning

In spindle turning, the work is supported between the centers of the headstock and tailstock. This set-up is used to turn cylindrical shapes like the lamp bases shown in figure 33-2.

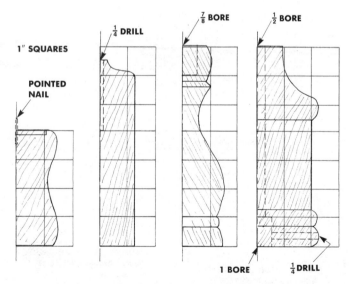

Figure 33-2: Cylinderical shapes are turned on the lathe by setting the work between the headstock and tailstock.

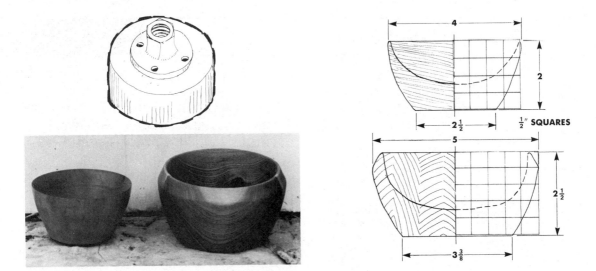

Figure 33-3: The face plate is a flat steel disk that can be mounted on the headstock. Bowls are made by screwing wood to the face plate.

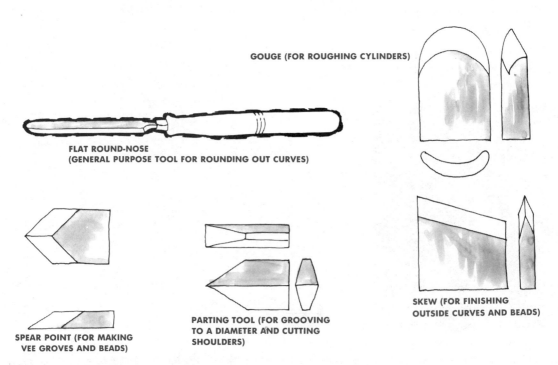

GOUGE (FOR ROUGHING CYLINDERS)

FLAT ROUND-NOSE
(GENERAL PURPOSE TOOL FOR ROUNDING OUT CURVES)

SPEAR POINT (FOR MAKING
VEE GROVES AND BEADS)

PARTING TOOL (FOR GROOVING
TO A DIAMETER AND CUTTING
SHOULDERS)

SKEW (FOR FINISHING
OUTSIDE CURVES AND BEADS)

Figure 33-4: Shaping of wood on a lathe is done with chisels.

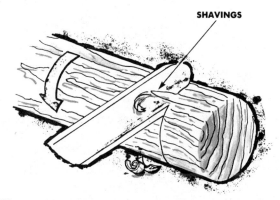

SHAVINGS

Figure 33-5: Shearing the wood leaves a smooth surface that requires little sanding.

Figure 33-6: Finely sheared wood is usually done by experts.

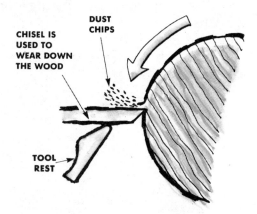

CHISEL IS USED TO WEAR DOWN THE WOOD

DUST CHIPS

TOOL REST

Figure 33-7: Scraping is an alternate method to shearing.

In <u>face plate turning</u>, the work is attached to the headstock end of the lathe only. It is screwed to a flat steel disk called a face plate. Bowls like those shown in figure 33-3 are made this way.

The lathe spins the wood. The worker shapes the wood with various kinds of chisels as it spins (figure 33-4). There are two methods of doing this. Expert woodworkers shear the wood (figure 33-5). The result is a smooth surface that needs little sanding (figure 33-6). The scraping method (figure 33-7) leaves rougher surfaces (figures 33-8 and 33-9), but it is the safest and easiest method for the beginner to learn.

There are a lot of chances for accidents when using a lathe and all safety rules should be followed (figure 33-10).

Figure 33-8: Scraping leaves a rougher surface than shearing, but it is easier to do at first.

Firuge 33-9: Softwoods scrape poorly, but this turning could have been improved by using sharp tools and light cuts.

- DRESS RIGHT, WEAR EYE PROTECTION, TUCK IN LOOSE CLOTHING AND HAIR.

- TURN ONLY GOOD WOOD. IT MUST BE FREE OF KNOTS, CRACKS AND POOR GLUE JOINTS.

- ALWAYS START TURNINGS AT THE SLOWEST SPEED. HAVE YOUR INSTRUCTOR SET THE CORRECT SPEED FOR YOU.

- BEFORE TURNING ON THE POWER, ROTATE THE WORK BY HAND TO BE SURE IT DOES NOT STRIKE THE TOOL REST.

- DO NOT FORCE TOOLS. IF THEY DO NOT CUT EASILY, THEY ARE DULL.

- KEEP TURNING CHISELS SHARP. REQUEST INSTRUCTOR'S ASSISTANCE WHEN CHISELS NEED SHARPENING.

- ALWAYS KEEP BOTH HANDS ON THE CHISEL.

Figure 33-10: Following safety rules for the lathe is important.

Figure 33-11: A face shield is recommended for all wood turners.

SELF CHECK

1. What are the four major parts of the lathe?
2. List the two types of turning done with the lathe?
3. How are bowls turned?
4. What is the difference between shearing and scraping?

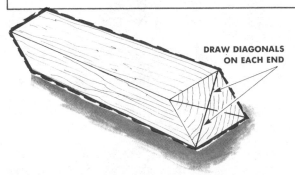

Figure 34-1: A turning square should be about the same size in thickness and in width.

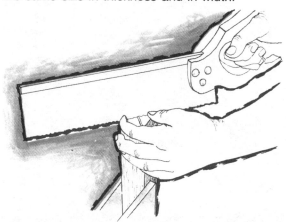

Figure 34-2: Saw cuts are made in the stock to take the spur-center.

Use of the lathe involves the steps from putting the stock on the lathe to final finishing. The basic steps are:

● Preparing the stock
● Mounting the stock between centers
● Adjusting the tool rest
● Rough turning
● Parting
● Turning coves, vees, and beads
● Sanding

Preparing the stock starts with selecting good turning stock. The thickness and width should be about the same dimension (figure 34-1). Make two saw cuts (about one-eighth inch deep) in one end (figure 34-2). If the workpiece is more than two inches square, remove the corners (figure 34-3) with a hand plane or the band saw. If necessary, remove the spur-center from the lathe (figure 34-4).

Drive the spur-center into the end of the stock with the saw cuts (figure 34-5). Use a mallet. A regular steel ham-

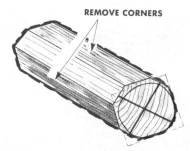

Figure 34-3: When the work piece is more than 2 inches square, the corners should be removed with a plane or saw.

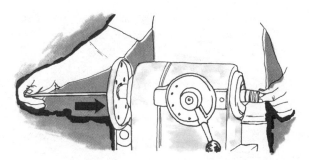

Figure 34-4: The spur-center (live-center) may be removed from the lathe for mounting.

Figure 34-5: Do not use a steel hammer to drive the spur-center into the saw cuts. It will damage the spur-center.

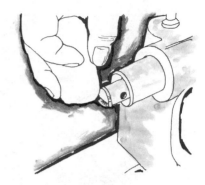

Figure 34-6: Mounting the stock between centers begins with lubricating the dead-center with bar soap or stick wax.

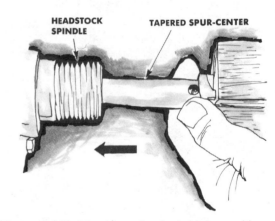

Figure 34-7: The piece is placed into position.

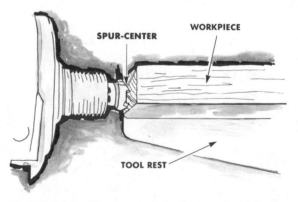

Figure 34-8: The spur-center is inserted into the headstock spindle.

mer will squash the tapered end of the spur center.

To mount stock between centers, lubricate the dead-center (figure 34-6). Insert the spur-center into the tapered opening of the headstock spindle (figures 34-7 and 34-8). The spur-center is also called the live-center. Slide the tailstock into position and clamp it to the bed (figure 34-9). Advance the dead-center into the work end (figure 34-10). Turn it in about one-sixteenth inch and lock it.

Adjust the tool rest as shown in figure 34-11. It should be about one-

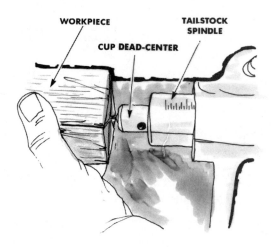

Figure 34-9: Slide the tailstock into position and clamp it to the bed.

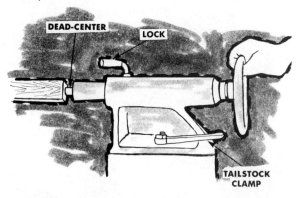

Figure 34-10: Advance the tailstock dead-center into the work and lock the spindle.

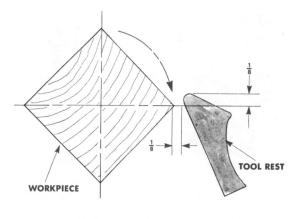

Figure 34-11: The tool rest is set about 1/8 inch from the corners of the stock.

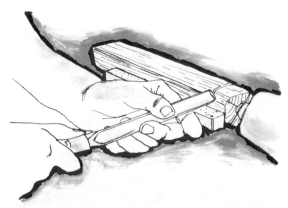

Figure 34-12: When rough turning with the gouge, cut toward the ends. Hold the gouge as shown so chips will be thrown away from you.

eighth inch from the corners of the stock as the work is rotated by hand. Adjust the vertical height of the tool rest so that it is about one-eighth inch above a horizontal center. Lock both adjustments firmly.

For rough turning, double check all adjustments, and review the general safety rules in Unit 33. If everything is ready, turn on the power. Use a large

gouge for roughing off the corners. Be sure the gouge is placed on the tool rest before it touches the wood. Figure 34-12 shows how to use the gouge. As the corners are removed, stop the power and readjust the tool rest. Turn until the stock is round.

The parting tool (figure 34-13) is used to square ends, make shoulders, and to plot out various diameters. Use

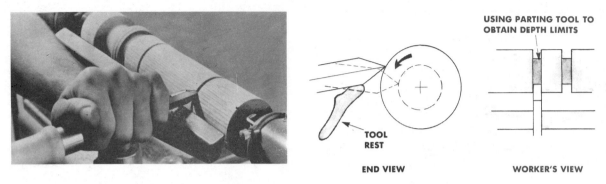

Figure 34-13: The parting tool is used to square ends and make shoulders.

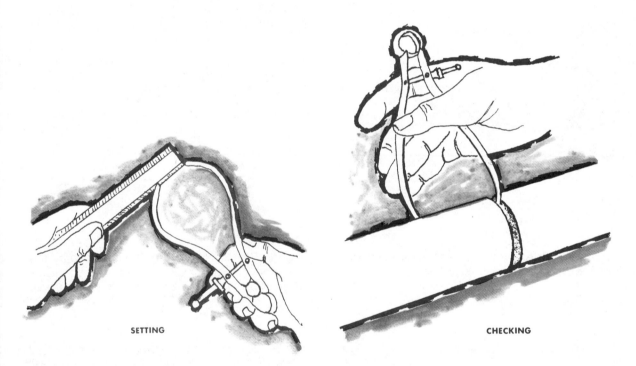

Figure 34-14: Calipers make it possible to check diameters while the work is on the lathe. Do not make measurements while the lathe is running.

calipers (figure 34-14) for checking diameters. Remember to allow some extra thickness for sanding.

Scraping vees and beads is done with the spear-point chisel (figure 34-15).

All scraping tools are used with the bevel down. The round-nose chisel (figure 34-16) is used to make inside curves called coves. When scraping any shape, always try to work "downhill"

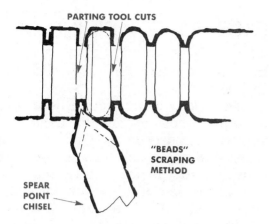

Figure 34-15: Vees and beads are made with a spear-point chisel.

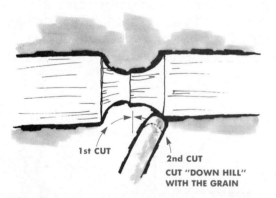

Figure 34-16: Inside curves, called coves, are formed with the round-nose chisel.

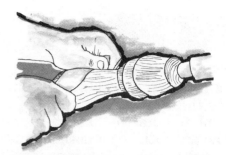

Figure 34-17: To sand large curves and flats, use a strip of sandpaper across the top of the work.

Figure 34-18: A folded pad of sandpaper is held under the work to sand inside curves.

the grain, so use fine grit paper. For the final work, stop the lathe and sand out cross-grain scratches by hand—working with the grain.

with the grain. Compare it to sharpening a pencil with a knife. Cut toward the end, not toward the center.

<u>Sanding on the lathe</u> is done with the work rotating under power. When sanding, always remove the tool rest and wear a dust mask and goggles. Use a strip of sandpaper held over the top (figure 34-17) or a folded pad held under the work (figure 34-18). Sanding with the lathe under power is across

---

SELF CHECK

1. What is used to lubricate the dead-center?
2. Which tool is used to "knock off" the corners in rough turning?
3. Can the tool rest be adjusted with the power on?
4. Which tool is used to measure spindle diameters?

FACE PLATE TURNING

Figure 35-1 shows the steps to prepare stock for face plate turning. Remove the spur-center, and thread the face plate onto the headstock spindle.

The tailstock is not normally used for face plate turning. However it is a good idea for beginners to run the tailstock dead-center against the work (figure 35-2). This is an added safety measure. Keep it there until the outside has been turned true and the stock is evenly balanced.

Observe all of the precautions described in Units 33 and 34. Adjust the tool rest to about one-eighth inch above the horizontal center. Rotate the work

by hand to make certain it clears the tool rest.

Use a skew or flat round-nose chisel on the outside to true the band sawn surfaces (figure 35-3). Once they are true, stop the machine and move the tailstock to the far right. Beginners should not use a gouge on face plate work. It is difficult to control. It often catches and digs into the work.

Use a round-nose chisel for hollowing out the inside (figure 35-4). Always try to cut with the grain. Use a sharp skew to finish scraping flat surfaces (figure 35-5) and outside curves. A sharp round-nose chisel (with a light

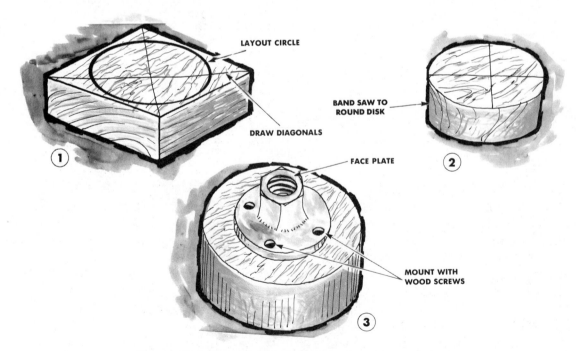

Figure 35-1: Readying the stock for face plate turning.

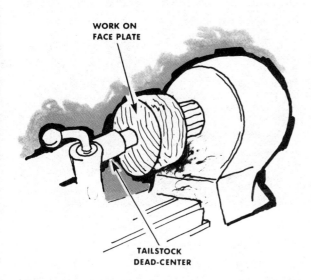

Figure 35-2: Using the tailstock to steady the workpieces until the stock is evenly balanced is a safety practice.

Figure 35-3: The outside is turned with a skew.

Figure 35-4: A round-nose chisel is used to hollow out the inside.

cut) is used to smooth inside curves. The face plate work is completed by sanding (figure 35-6) and as described in Unit 34.

Figure 35-5: The skew makes light scraping cuts on a flat surface.

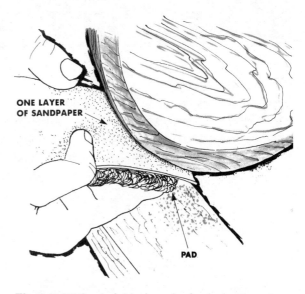

Figure 35-6: A folded pad of sandpaper completes the work.

SELF CHECK

1. What machine is used to saw the stock round before it is mounted in the lathe?
2. What is used to attach the wood to the face plate?
3. What purpose does the tailstock dead-center serve for beginning face plate turners?
4. Which tool is used to true an outside surface?

WOOD AND WOOD MATERIALS

7

The woodworker builds projects from wood. These projects may be as simple and as beautiful as a book end, or they may be as complicated and rugged as a home or a boat. Any competent woodworker must be able to choose the correct material as well as the correct tool to do the job.

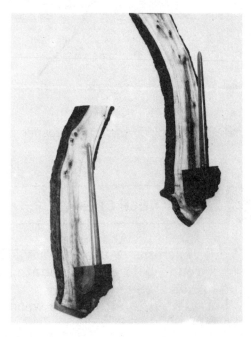

RUSTIC CANDLE SCONCES are made from a tree branch cut lengthwise. The holders are end grain slabs from the same branch. Treat in PEG (polyethylene glycol) to keep the bark firmly attached.(Spielman's Wood Works)

BENT RING TRINKET SHELF shown in ash is an experiment in bending wood. Saw kerf the slots in the base with the band saw. Select straight grain veneer. If it does not bend easily, soak it in hot water for ten minutes. Bend quickly—set in slots to dry.

THE NATURE OF WOOD

Wood is an interesting material. It is very complex in structure. To use wood wisely, skilled woodworkers know what certain kinds of wood will and will not do. It is a matter of control. Skilled woodworkers know the good and the bad properties of wood for certain uses (figure 36-1). They control the end result by making the best choice.

There are good reasons why baseball bats and birdhouses are not made from the same wood. Studying this Unit will help you to know why.

The structure of wood is determined by its growth. A tree puts on a new layer every year (figure 36-2). Each new layer (shell) adds another line to the grain. Wood consists of long, hol-

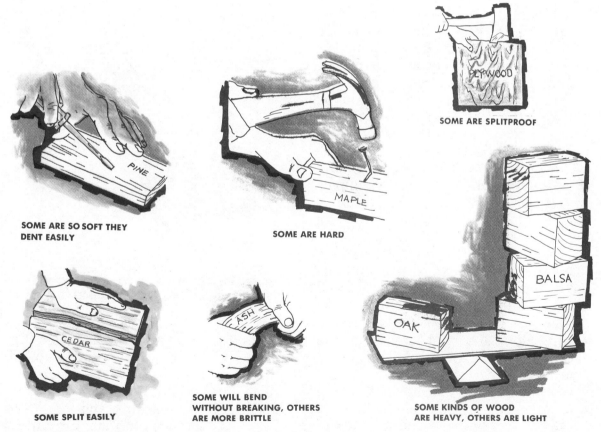

SOME ARE SO SOFT THEY DENT EASILY

SOME ARE HARD

SOME ARE SPLITPROOF

SOME SPLIT EASILY

SOME WILL BEND WITHOUT BREAKING, OTHERS ARE MORE BRITTLE

SOME KINDS OF WOOD ARE HEAVY, OTHERS ARE LIGHT

Figure 36-1: Knowing the qualities of the wood being used is as important as using the right tools.

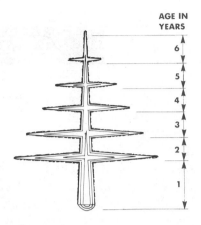

Figure 36-2: Rings in wood are added each year. They are growth layers.

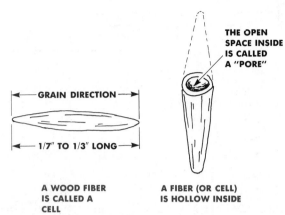

Figure 36-3: Wood consists of long, hollow, small, tough fibers (cells).

low, but very small and tough fibers (figure 36-3). Fibers are also called cells. They are glued together in parallel directions by nature's own glue within the tree. It is easier for woodworkers to cut or separate wood by splitting the fibers apart lengthwise than it is to cut across them (figure 36-4).

The <u>grain or fiber direction</u> should be considered where strength is important (figure 36-5). A general rule is that the heavier the wood is, the stronger it also is.

Like humans, all wood is not perfect. Some things about wood can discourage beginners. If you do not select and plan carefully, a hard knot may show up just where a nail is to be driven. Nailing close to a knot may crack the wood. To some people, knots are beautiful.

A nice table top might twist or cup if the wood has not been properly dried or cured for the air (and humidity) where the table will be used. Remem-

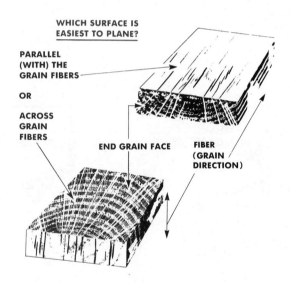

Figure 36-4: It is easier to cut wood with the grain. Grain varies from one wood to another.

ber that wood is just like a sponge (figure 36-7). A dry sponge will absorb water in its pores. A wet sponge will shrivel and shrink if left in a dry room. Wood will swell, shrink and may even crack with changes in moisture unless it is properly cured.

Green wood, direct from the tree, is cured in three different ways:

● Kiln drying—the wood is dried in large special ovens. This type of wood is best for fine furniture and indoor projects.

● Air drying—the boards are stacked outside with air spaces between them.

This type of wood is okay for outdoor projects but it may warp and crack if used indoors.

● Chemical seasoning—the wood is treated with polyethylene glycol. It does not dry the wood at all. The chemical fills the fibers (cells) so the wood does not take on (or lose) moisture. Chemically seasoned wood is good for natural thick pieces used for indoor projects (figure 36-8).

Identifying different kinds of wood takes a lot of effort and practice. Grain (texture and pattern) is one identifying factor. The pores on some woods such as oak, ash, mahogany, and walnut are actually visible. Color is another key to identification. Redwood is reddish, and black walnut is a dark brown. Pine, birch, maple, basswood, oak, and ash are all light in color.

Physical hardness is a third aid to identifying different kinds of wood. Some of the hardest wood includes oak, cherry, birch, maple, and ash. Softer woods include pine, basswood, willow, cedar and redwood. Mahogany and butternut are medium hard.

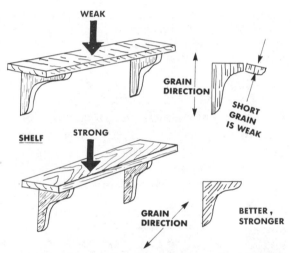

Figure 36-5: Heavier wood is usually stronger. It is harder to break the fibers that make up wood grain than to split them.

Figure 36-6: If wood isn't properly dried it may warp.

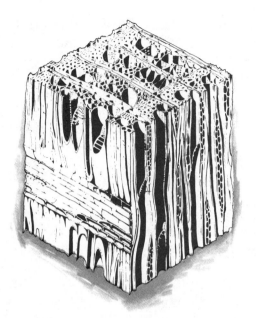

Figure 36-8: This clock is made from wood that has been "cured" with chemicals. The chemical treatment stops it from shrinking, cracking, or expanding.(Spielman's Wood Works)

Figure 36-7: Wood is porous. When it is enlarged it looks like a sponge.

Two other "keys" to identifying woods are <u>weight and smell</u>. Pine is light in weight compared to maple but they are about the same color. Both pine shavings and cedar wood have a distinctive odor.

Observe common usage to learn which kind of wood is used for certain reasons. Fir and spruce are not normally used for furniture. Because of their strength and nail holding qualities, they are used for framing members inside the walls of homes. Walnut is a common gun stock and fine furniture wood. Ash is good for baseball bats and water skis because it is hard and tough, yet not brittle. Wood carvers like certain woods. Carpenters use only a few special species. Boat builders and furniture makers have their choices.

SELF CHECK

1. Are all woods alike in their performance?
2. Is it easier to cut wood with the fibers or across the fibers?
3. Why is grain direction an important consideration for strength?
4. Why do wood and sponges react to moisture in the same ways?

WOOD SHEET MATERIALS

Some of the problems of working with solid wood boards can be eliminated by using wood sheet materials. Sheet materials come in large flat panels with less tendency to warp. They can be less expensive, stronger, and almost as beautiful as solid wood. Most sheet materials are free of knots and they are not as likely to split. The three basic wood sheet materials are:

● Plywood
● Particle board
● Hardboard

Plywood (figure 37-1) is a wood panel made by gluing thin layers of wood (veneer) together at right angles to form a sheet. Veneers are cut in one piece from a log (figure 37-2). Hardwood plywoods are used in cabinets, paneling, furniture, and where the

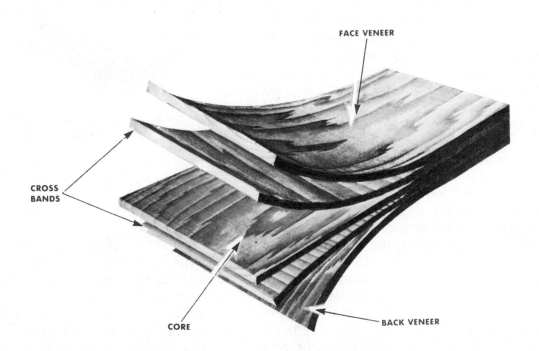

Figure 37-1: Plywood is made of layers of wood glued together. The grain runs at opposite angles in each layer.

wood will show. Softwood plywoods are used for construction where the wood is covered. Some softwood plywoods are used for the exposed exterior siding of homes. Less expensive softwood plywood is used for backs, bases, and non-exposed parts of furniture and cabinets.

Plywood can be purchased in indoor (interior) and outdoor (exterior) types. Cost varies with the thickness, kind of material, and grade (quality) of the face veneers. Full sheet plywood sizes are four feet wide and eight feet long. Common thicknesses range from one-quarter inch to three-quarter inch in one-eighth inch steps.

Particle board sheets (figure 37-3) are made from small chips (particles) of wood. Shavings, slivers, and chips are bonded together with resin glues under heat and pressure. Particle board has a poor appearance because of the way it is made. Its low cost and uniform hardness are advantages. But particle board dulls common edge cutting tools quickly because it contains so much resin glue. Standard sheet sizes are the same as plywood.

Hardboard is not made the same way as particle board. Chips are reduced to individual wood fibers. Then the fibers are pressed together under heat and pressure to make flat sheets. Hardboards are low in price and generally cheaper than plywoods. They are used for cabinet backs and drawer bottoms. Some hardboard has wood grain or other textures printed and pressed into its surfaces. Other hardboards are specially made for outdoor use. Common sheet sizes are four feet by eight feet with one-eighth to one-quarter inch thickness.

Figure 37-2: Veneers are cut off a log with a razor sharp knife. As the log is rolled, the knife moves to keep the wood sheet coming off like one piece of paper.

Figure 37-3: Particle board is made of pressed and glued panels of wood chips.

SELF CHECK

1. List three advantages sheet materials have over solid lumber.
2. List three basic kinds of wood sheet materials.
3. What are the standard width and length sizes of wood sheet materials?
4. Why does particle board dull edge cutting tools?

PROJECTS

8

Many projects are pictured and described on the following pages. Others are also found earlier in this book.

All of the projects in this book have been made in a shop such as yours. Each project has the easiest possible type of construction yet has good quality and appearance.

Some projects are very simple. These are still fun to make and own. Others are more complex. All the projects shown are within the range of the be-

ginner. Discuss project selections with your instructor. Be sure they fit into the limits of time, material and tool usage set for your class.

Only the most important information is provided. With most of the projects you will have to work out your own bill of materials and some construction details. For example, you will have to choose the best nail or screw sizes for joints.

CANDLE LAMP Use a face plate to turn the one and one-half by four and one-half inch diameter base. Purchase a glass chimney from a hardware store about eight and one-half inches high and two and one-half inches in diameter at the base. Cut a one-quarter inch deep slot for the glass chimney. Bore a seven-eighths by one inch deep hole for the candle.

HANGING OR STANDING PLANTER of stained ash is made of a three-quarter by seven inch diameter plywood bottom and these vertical slats:

Four pieces—one-half by seven-eighths by twelve

Twenty pieces—one-half by seven-eighths by eight

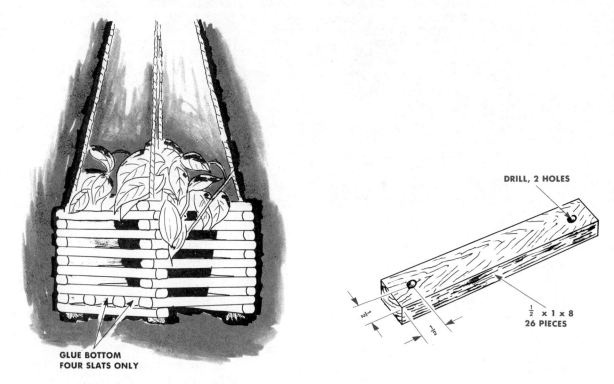

DRILL, 2 HOLES

$\frac{1}{2}$ x 1 x 8
26 PIECES

**GLUE BOTTOM
FOUR SLATS ONLY**

STICK PLANTER of stained ash is an exercise in production. All 26 pieces are alike. Devise ways for cutting to length and drilling the holes without marking each individual piece.

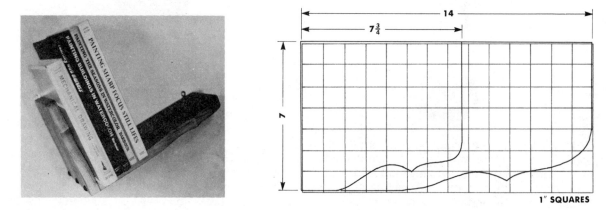

14

7 $\frac{3}{4}$

7

1" SQUARES

SLANTED BOOK SHELF in natural willow has a simple right angle butt joint. Strengthen with counterbored wood screws. Hide them with screw hole buttons or flush plugs.

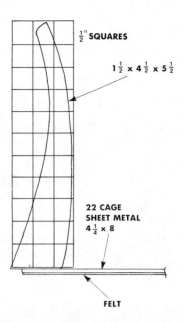

½" SQUARES

1 ½ x 4 ½ x 5 ½

22 CAGE
SHEET METAL
4 ¼ x 8

FELT

BOOK END of mahogany is band sawn to shape. Saw from one and one-half inch stock on edge. Fasten the sheet metal base with countersunk screws. Glue on felt to protect shelf or table surfaces.

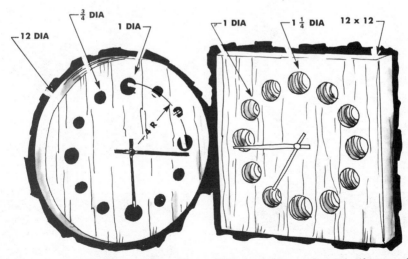

12 DIA

¾ DIA

1 DIA

1 DIA

1 ¼ DIA

12 x 12

CLOCKS of stained pine are easy to make. Use solid wood one and one-half to two inches thick. Rough out the opening for the movement (battery or electric) using a forstner bit on the drill press. Set the depth stop to control the depth. Finish off with a sharp chisel. Round all face edges with a one-quarter inch radius, piloted router bit.

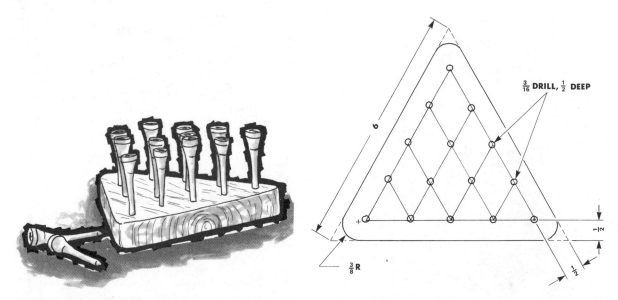

PEG JUMP PUZZLE of three-quarter inch butternut is a tricky layout job and a tricky game to play too. The 15 holes are laid out by repeating equilateral triangles. Purchase 14 golf tees for the pegs. Object of the game is to remove all pegs by jumping until only one is left.

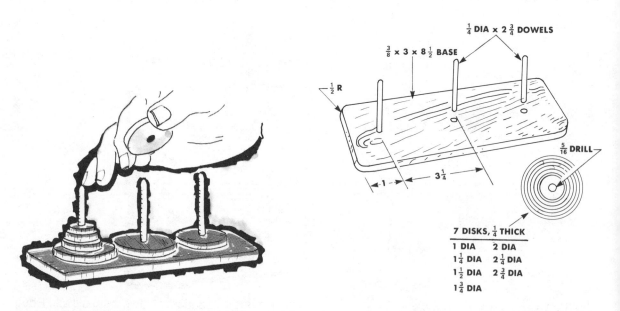

STACKING DISK PUZZLE uses contrasting woods such as walnut and maple. The object of the puzzle: move the seven disks from one post to another—one at a time. Never place a larger disk on a smaller one.

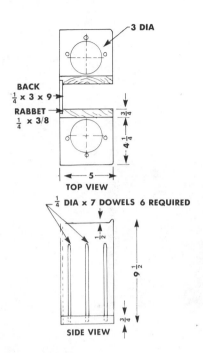

TENNIS GEAR HOLDER of natural pine has vertical rabbet joints for the back. Use butt joints for the ball supporting shelves.

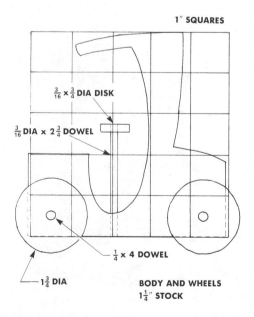

TOY CAR in unfinished pine. Drill five-sixteenths inch holes through the body for the wheel axles. Use one-quarter inch washers between the body and each wheel.

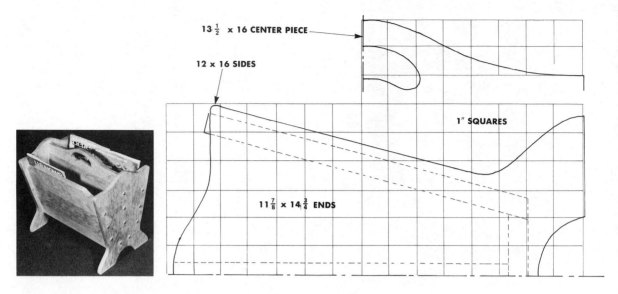

$13\frac{1}{2}$ x 16 CENTER PIECE

12 x 16 SIDES

1" SQUARES

$11\frac{7}{8}$ x $14\frac{3}{4}$ ENDS

MAGAZINE RACK of natural pine is made with all butt joints. Stack cut the ends on the band saw so both pieces are made alike. (by John Wehling)

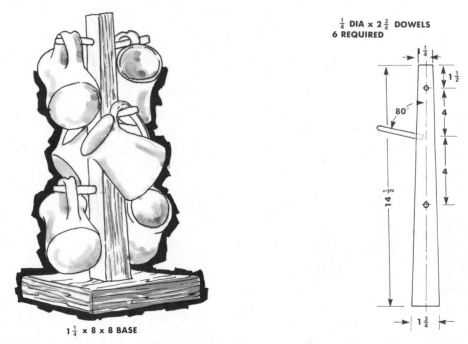

$\frac{1}{4}$ DIA x $2\frac{3}{4}$ DOWELS
6 REQUIRED

$\frac{1}{4}$

$1\frac{1}{2}$

$80°$

4

$14\frac{1}{2}$

4

$1\frac{3}{4}$

$1\frac{1}{4}$ x 8 x 8 BASE

MUG TREE of stained pine. Drill dowel holes before tapering with a hand plane. Assemble with glue and a large flat head wood screw.

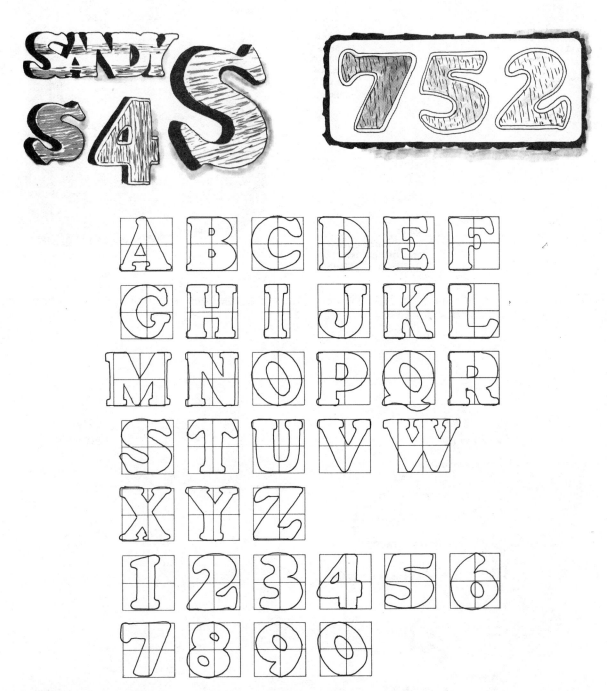

LETTERS AND NUMBERS can be made with solid lumber, as shown, or plywood. Imagine the ways you can use these designs. Run the letters together (overlap patterns) to make names. Make initial book ends, lamp bases or hang-ups to decorate a wall. House numbers should be made of smooth or rough sawn cedar or redwood. Enlarge the patterns to satisfy your needs.

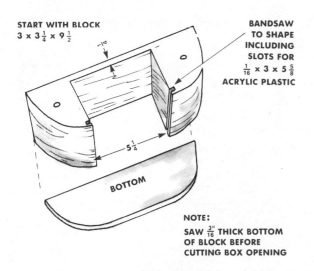

CARD FILE in natural pine holds 3x5 inch index cards. Saw the bottom off of the block before cutting to shape. Glue it back on after sawing and sanding.

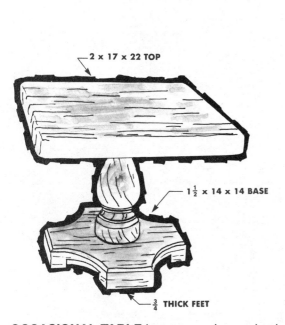

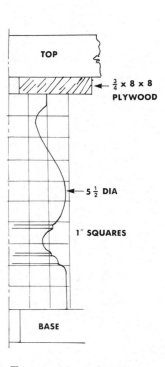

OCCASIONAL TABLE is a more advanced spindle turning project. Turn accurate dowel pegs one inch in diameter at both ends of the spindle. This will simplify assembly and add strength. (designed by Greg Swain)

SHUFFLE PUZZLE is made of walnut and maple blocks with a butternut frame. The task is to get the largest block out of the opening without lifting the other blocks.

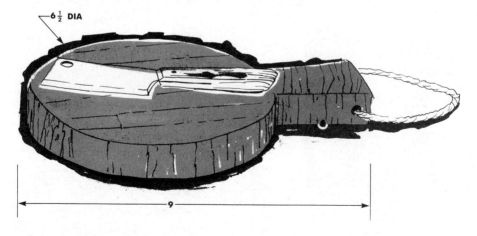

CHEESE BOARD If making from built-up stock, be sure to use a waterproof glue.

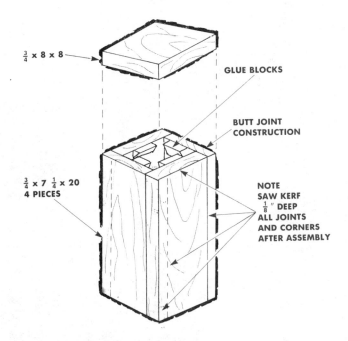

$\frac{3}{4}$ x 8 x 8

GLUE BLOCKS

BUTT JOINT CONSTRUCTION

$\frac{3}{4}$ x 7 $\frac{1}{4}$ x 20
4 PIECES

**NOTE
SAW KERF
$\frac{1}{8}$" DEEP
ALL JOINTS
AND CORNERS
AFTER ASSEMBLY**

PLANT STAND of willow is a good starting project for the table saw. Four identical pieces are assembled with butt joints to make a square column. Assemble with finish nails and glue. Reinforce with glue blocks. After assembly, make rip saw cuts one-eighth inch deep at the center of every joint. Make cuts (at the same setting) at each corner before fastening the top. Make a similar kerf crosscutting all around where the top meets the sides.

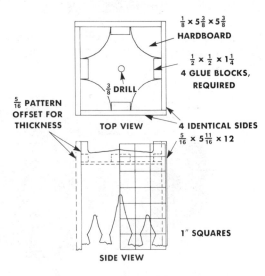

$\frac{1}{8}$ x 5 $\frac{3}{8}$ x 5 $\frac{3}{8}$
HARDBOARD

$\frac{1}{2}$ x $\frac{1}{2}$ x 1 $\frac{1}{4}$
**4 GLUE BLOCKS,
REQUIRED**

$\frac{3}{8}$ **DRILL**

$\frac{5}{16}$ **PATTERN
OFFSET FOR
THICKNESS**

TOP VIEW

4 IDENTICAL SIDES
$\frac{5}{16}$ x 5 $\frac{11}{16}$ x 12

1" SQUARES

SIDE VIEW

HANGING BOX LAMP of wormy butternut is made of four identical sides. Note the plan showing the off-set in the design for the butt joints.

GLOSSARY

Abrasives: Material used to smooth wood or grind metal by abrading.

Adhesive: The bonding material known as glue that is used to join pieces of wood together.

Air Dried: Boards dried outdoors, in stacks, with spacers between each piece to provide free air movement. Abbreviation: A.D.

Auger: A carpenters tool used for boring holes.

Band saw: A fast cutting machine with an endless (band) blade used to cut straight lines and curves in thicker wood.

Bevel: An angle cut edge.

Bill of Materials: A list of everything needed to make a project.

Bit: Refers to cutting tools used for drilling and routing.

Block Plane: A small hand tool used to remove thin shavings from wood. It is designed for working end grain surfaces, but has other uses.

Board Foot: One hundred forty four cubic inches of a board calculated from its rough sawn thickness.

Boring: The process of using an auger bit to cut holes larger than one-quarter inch in diameter in wood.

Brace: A carpenters hand tool used to hold and turn various bits (such as auger bits).

Butt: The simplest of right angle joints.

Cell: A wood fiber.

Chamfer: Result of making an angle cut between the face and edge or end of a piece of wood.

Chuck: The part of a drill, brace or jig saw that holds or clamps the cutting tool or blade.

Chuck Key: A gear tooth device for tightening bits in drill chucks.

Close Grain: Refers to woods with very fine fibers or cells that are not visibly porous.

Crosscut: A kind of saw, or the operation of sawing across the grain of wood to make a specific length.

Cup: Type of warpage in which the board is bent hollow across the grain.

Cutterhead: The part of a jointer or surface planer that carries the knives that do the cutting.

Cutting bevel: The surface of a cutting tool which is made by grinding to produce an edge for shearing or slicing wood.

Dado: A slot wider than a saw cut. A dado is made across the grain.

Dead Center: The part of the lathe tail stock on which the work rotates or pivots. Also known as a cup center.

Drill: A tool or the process of cutting holes less than one-quarter inch in diameter.

Easing An Edge: To reduce the sharp square corners of a board by sanding lightly to a small radius.

Edge: One of three surfaces of a board.

Epoxy: A type of glue, which consists of two parts that must be measured and mixed. Expensive, but waterproof.

Expansive Bit: An adjustable tool for boring holes of various diameters.

Face: Usually the largest of the three surfaces of a board.

Face Plate: Part of a lathe that holds the work for turning bowls and similar objects.

Feed: Usually refers to a direction for advancing a tool to the wood or advancing the wood into a machine.

Fence: A guide on band saws, table saws and jointers used to guide the wood.

Fiber: The fine tube-like structure of wood which is hollow and determines the grain direction.

Forstner Bit: A special boring tool that cuts holes with flat bottoms.

Gouge: A chisel-like tool with a curved cutting edge.

Grit: The coarseness or smoothness of sandpaper or abrasives such as fine grit or coarse grit sandpaper.

Groove: A slot wider than a saw cut made parallel to the grain.

Hand Screw: A clamp easily identified as the type with wooden jaws.

Hardboard: A sheet material made from chips of wood reduced to individual fibers and then pressed into panels.

Honing: The final process of sharpening a bevel edge tool on a flat oil stone.

Jig Saw: A machine with a thin blade that moves up and down for sawing curves in wood. Also known as a scroll saw.

Joint: The fitting together of two or more pieces of wood.

Jointer: A hand fed machine used to plane the edges and faces of boards by means of a rotating cutting head with three knives.

Kerf: The path cut by a saw.

Kiln Dried: Wood cured or seasoned in a special oven. Abbreviated as K.D.

Lap Joint: Name given to several types of joints in which half the thickness of each piece is cut away. End lap, corner lap and cross lap are typical lap joints.

Lead: The tendency of a tool to follow the grain rather than the desired direction.

Miter Gauge: A device which the wood is held against for crosscutting on a table saw or band saw.

Mortise and Tenon: A type of right angle joint found on advanced furniture and cabinet projects.

Nail Set: A tool used to drive finishing nails below the surface.

Open Grain: Refers to the kinds of wood with larger pores or cells.

Particle Board: A sheet material made by pressing chips and resins together with heat and pressure to form large panels.

Penny: A term used to describe the sizes of nails and abbreviated as the letter "d".

Phillips Head: Refers to a type of screw with cross slots in the screw head.

Pilot: The part of a router bit which guides and controls the horizontal feed of a router.

Pilot Hole: A special hole made for the thread part of a wood screw.

Push Stick: A safety device used to feed wood into machines. It allows you to keep your hands a safe distance away from the cutter or blade.

Plane: The tool or the process of reducing wood by removing thin shavings with a knife like cutter.

Plane Iron: The cutting part of a hand plane.

Plywood: Sheet material made by gluing thin layers of wood or veneer together with the grain of each layer running at right angles to each other.

Rabbet: An L-shaped cut along an edge or end of a board.

Rasp: A very coarse (fast cutting) file.

Relief Cut: Short straight cuts made at right angles to a curved layout line so sharper than normal curves can be cut with the jig or band saw.

Resawing: Cutting to thickness with a band or table saw.

Rip: A kind of saw or operation of sawing with the grain to make a certain width.

Rout: Cutting or forming with special bits into the edges, ends or face of wood.

Saber Saw: A portable electric tool used for sawing straight lines and curves in wood.

Scraping Method: One way of turning in which the chisels are applied to the work to wear down the wood.

Scroll Saw: See Jig Saw.

Set: The alternate outward bending of saw teeth so they cut a path wider than the blade thickness.

Shank: The part of a drill, auger bit or router bit held in a chuck.

Shank Clearance Hole: A special size hole made in wood so the unthreaded part of a wood screw just slip fits into it.

Sheet Material: Any wood or plastic materials made in flat panels.

Skew: A type of chisel used in wood turning.

Socket Chisel: The design of a chisel in which the handle fits into a cone shaped opening (or socket).

Spindle Turning: Work which is held between the two centers of a lathe.

Spur: A part of a boring tool designed to sever the grain fibers with a knife-point like cutting action.

Spur-Center: A part of the lathe in the headstock that grips the work and turns it. Also known as the live-center.

Stack Cutting: Sawing several pieces at one time when all are held together with nails or other fasteners.

S2S: Refers to lumber that has been reduced from rough to surfaced smooth on two sides.

Surfacer or Surface Planer: An advanced power feed machine used to plane stock to a parallel thickness.

Tang: The part of a chisel or auger bit opposite the cutting end.

Taper: An edge or surface of a board that does not run parallel with the opposite edge.

Templet: A full size pattern of a shape or part. Usually made of thin, rigid sheet material.

Veneer: Thin slices or sheets of wood.

Warp: Distorted lumber, such as twist, cup, or bow.

Worked Lumber: Any solid wood materials that have been milled into special shapes, such as dowels and mouldings.

A

Abrasives, 65
Acrylic plastic, 93-95
Aerosol spray finishes, 89, 92
Air drying wood, 120
Aluminum oxide, 65
Animal feed supplement, 1
Ash, 120, 121
Auger bits, 43, 44, 45

B

Backsaw, 19, 20
Band saw, 30-33, 34-37
Band saw blades, sharpening, 63
Bar clamps, 80, 81
Basswood, 120
Beads, scraping, 113, 114
Belt sanders, 70-71
Belt sanding machines, 72
Bevel ripping, 34
Bevels, planing, 40, 41, 42
Bill of materials, 13
Birch, 120
Birdhouse project, 35-36
Bits
  auger, 43, 44, 45
  expansive, 43,44
  forstner, 50
  multi-spur, 50
  router, 56-69
Black walnut, 120
Blade
  band saw, 30, 63
  jigsaw, 26
Block plane, 40
Block planing, 41-42
Board feet, 10-11
Boards, 10
Book end project, 126
Boring, hand, 43-45
Boring tools 50, 62-63
Box lamp project, 88
Box nails, 82
Brace, hand, 43, 44
Brushes, caring for, 89, 92
Butternut, 120
Butt joints, 76

C

Cabinets, 1
Calipers, 112-113
Candle cups, 93, 94
Candle holders projects, 96
Candle lamp project, 124, 125
Candle sconce project, 88
Card file project, 131
C-clamps, 80, 81
Cedar, 120, 121

Cells, wood, 119
Center line, 9
Chamfers
  planing, 40, 41, 42
  with sanders, 74
Cheese board project, 132
Cherry, 120
Chisels, 52-53, 107, 108
  grinding, 61
Chuck keys, 46
Clamping, 80-81
Clock project, 126
Clothes rack, 6, 9
Collars for drilling, 48
Color of wood, 120
Combination square, 14, 15
Common nails, 82
Complex cuts, 31, 32
Compound band sawing, 36-37
Coping saw, 22, 23
Corn oil, 91
Coves, 113, 114
Crosscutting, 20, 21, 33
  with table saw, 98
Crosscut saw teeth, 19
Cupped stock, 103
Curves
  cutting, 22-23
  sanding, 68, 69, 72, 73
Cuts, complex, 27-29, 31, 32
Cutting boards project, 75
Cutting wood, 18-37

D

Dado joints, 77, 78
Dadoes, 56, 57, 58
Dents in wood, raising, 69
Depth stop, drill, 50-51
Dimensions line, 9
Dimensions in a drawing, 9
Dimensions of lumber, 11, 12
Disk sanders, 72
Double cut file, 54
Double insulated drills, 47
Dovetail saw, 19, 20-21
Drawing
  straight line, 13
  project, 6-9
Drilling, 86
  hand, 43
  portable electric, 46-48
Drill press, 49-51
Drills
  double insulated, 47
  grounded, 46,47
  sharpening, 63
  twist, 43

  variable speed, 47-48
Drum sanders, 72-73
Drying wood, 120

E

Edge forming with router, 56, 57, 59
Edge jointing, 101-103
Edges, planing, 39, 40
End grain, 69
  planing, 40, 41-42
Epoxy glue, 79, 80
Expansive bits, 43, 44
Extension line, 9
Eye protection, 4, 5

F

Face jointing, 103
Face plate turning, 106-108, 115-116
Fastening wood, 75-87
Felt, 94, 95
Fence
  drill, 51
  ripping, 31-32, 33
  table saw, 98
Fibers, wood, 118-119
File card,
File project, 131
Files, 54-55
Finishes
  aerosol spray, 89, 92
  indoor, 89
  outdoor, 92
Finishing nails, 82, 83
Finishing wood, 88-95
Fir, 121
Flat file, 54, 55
Flint, 65
Foot bench rulers, 13
Forming tools, 54, 55
Forstner bit, 50
Frame for photo, 7
Framing square, 14, 15
Fuels, 1
Furniture, 1

G

Gaging a line, 13
Garnet, 65
Gluing, 79-81
Gouge, 52, 53, 112
Grain, wood, 19, 118-119
Green wood, 120
Grid system of drawing, 7-8
Grinders, 60
Grinding, freehand, 61
Grit, 65-66, 73
Groove forming with router, 56, 59
Grounded drills, 46, 47
Guard, table saw, 99, 100

Guns, 1
Gunsmith, 1

H

Half-round file, 54, 55
Hammers, 82, 83-84
Hand brace, 43, 44
Handles, file, 54
Handling of materials 4, 5
Hand planes, 38-40
Hands, protection, 54
Handsaws, 19-23, 63
Hangers, 93, 94
Hardboard, 123
Hardness of wood, 120
Hardware, 93-95
Hardwoods, 10
Heads of screws, 85, 86
Hidden line, 9
Holder project (for tennis gear), 128
Hone, 60, 62
Horseplay and safety, 4
Housekeeping, 4, 5

J

Jack plane, 38
Jewelry, 1
Jigsaw, 26-29
Jigs for drilling, 48
Jointer, 101-103
Joint fitting with router, 56, 57
Jointing
    edge, 101-103
    face, 103
Joints, 76-78

K

Kerf, 19, 20, 21-22, 25
Kiln drying wood, 120
Knots in wood, 119

L

Lamp parts, 95
Lap joints 78
Lathe, 106-111
Letter opener, 7
Letters projects 130
Linear foot, 12, 13
Lines, drawing, 9
Liquid glue, 79
Lumber, 10

M

Machines for woodworking,
    advanced, 96-116
Magazine rack project, 129
Mahogany, 120
Maple, 120
Materials, 4, 5, 10-12
Material storage 4, 5

Measuring, 9, 13
    metric, 14-15, 16
Miter box, 22
Miter gage attachment, 33
Miter gage clamp, 99-100
Miter joints, 76, 77
Miters with sanders, 74
Mortise and tenon joints, 78
Mouldings, 10
Mug rack, 6, 8
Mug tree project 129
Multi-spur bit, 50

N

Nailing, 82-84
Natural abrasives, 65
Nibble cuts, 32
Numbers project, 130

O

Oak, 120
Oils, finishing, 91
Olive oil, 91

P

Pad sanders, 70
Paper, 1
Particle board, 123
Parting tool, 112-113
Peanut oil, 91
Personal safety, 4
Phillip's head screws, 85-86
Picture frames project, 64
Pilot holes, 86
Pine, 120, 121
Planer, surface, 104-105
Planes, hand, 38-40
Planing
    block, 41-42
    jointer, 101-103
    surface, 104-105
    wood, 38-42
Planter project, 124
Plant hanger project, 88
Plant stand project, 133
Plastics, 1, 93-95
Plywood, 10, 21, 122-123
Powder glue, 79
Project, planning, 6-9
Protection
    eye, 4, 5
    hands, 31
Protective felt, 94, 95
Puzzle projects, 127, 132
Push stick, 103

R

Rabbets, 56, 57, 58, 76-78
Racks, 6, 8-9

Rasps, 54
Rat tail file, 54, 55
Redwood, 120
Relief cuts, 31, 33
Resawing, 34
Ripping, 21
    bevel, 34
    slice, 34-35
    on table saw, 97-98
Ripping fence, 31-32, 33
Ripsaws, 19
Ripsaw teeth, 19, 20
Rough lumber, 10
Rounding corners with sander, 74
Round-nose chisel, 113, 114, 115-116
Round table project, 96
Router, 56-59
Router bits, sharpening, 63
Rulers, 13
Running foot, 12

S

Saber saws, 24-25
Safety, 4-5
    band saw, 30, 31
    chisels, 52
    drill press, 50
    files, 55
    grinder, 60
    jigsaw, 28
    jointer, 101, 102
    lathe, 108-109, 116
    personal, 4
    power equipment, 24
    router, 56, 58
    sanders, 70
    surface planer, 104, 105
    table saw, 98-100
Safety in resawing, 34
Sanding
    hand, 67-79
    portable electric, 70-71
Sanding block, 68, 69
Sanding machines, 72-74
Sanding on lathe, 114, 116
Sandpaper, 65-66
Saws
    saber, 24-25
    table, 97-100
Scale of drawing, 8-9
Scraping tools, 113-114
Scraping wood, 108
Scratch awl, 16
Screw clamps, 80, 81
Screwdriver, 87
Screw eyes and hooks, 93
Screws, 85-87

Scroll saw, 26-29
Sculpture, 1
Section drawings, 9
Sharpening planes, 39, 40
Shearing wood, 108
Sheet materials, 10, 12-13
Sheets, wood, 122-123
Shelf project, 18, 117, 125
Shingles, 36
Silicon carbide, 65
Single cut file, 54
Skew, 115, 116
Skills, woodworking, 2, 3
Ski rack, 6, 8
Slice ripping, 34-35
Slots, screw, 85-86
Smell of wood, 121
Smoothing wood, 64-75
Smooth plane, 38
Socket chisels, 52
Softwoods, 10
Spear-point chisel, 115, 116
Spindles, turning, 106, 110-114
Spruce, 121
Spur-center, 110-111
Spurs, 62-63
Square, 14, 22
Squaring a line, 13
Stains, applying, 90-91, 92
Stack cutting, 28, 29
Storage of materials, 4, 5
Surfaced four sides (S4S) lumber, 10
Surfaced two sides (S2S) lumber, 10

Surface planer, 104-105
Surfaces, planing, 40
Synthetic abrasives, 65

T
Table project, 131
Table saw, 97-100
Tailstock, 111-112
   lathe, 115
Tang chisels, 52
Tape measure, 13
Tapers, planing, 40
T-bevel, sliding, 15
Teeth, saw, 19
Templates, 14, 16, 36
Tennis racket holder, 8
Tennis racket rack, 6
Tongue and groove joints, 78
Tool rest, lathe, 111-112
Tools, measuring, 13
Toothpick, 1
Toy car project, 128
Try square, 14
Turning, face plate, 106-108, 115-116
Turning spindles, 106, 110-114
Turning stock, 110
Twist drills, 43

V
Variable speed drills, 47-48
Vees, scraping, 113, 114
Views, 9

W
Walnut, 120, 121
Warped stock, 103
Warping, 120
Weed pots project, 96
Weight of wood, 121
Whale project, 18
Whet stone, 62
Willow, 120
Wing compass, 15
Wood
   chemical seasoning, 120, 121
   color of, 120
   drying, 120
   green, 120
   hardness of, 120
   identifying, 120
   nature of, 118-121
   smell of, 121
   tools, 1
   weight of, 121
Woodcarver, 2
Wood cells, 119
Wood fibers, 118-119
Wood filler, 69
Wood grain, 118-119
Wood paneling, 1
Wood sheet materials, 122-123
Woodworking, 1, 2-3
Worked lumber, 10, 12